American
Artists

GREAT ARTISTS OF THE WESTERN WORLD

American Artists

James McNeill Whistler

— ❧ —

Mary Cassatt

— ❧ —

John Singer Sargent

— ❧ —

Edward Hopper

MARSHALL CAVENDISH · LONDON · NEW YORK · SYDNEY

Staff Credits

Editors	Clive Gregory LL B Sue Lyon BA (Honours)	**Picture Researchers**	Vanessa Fletcher BA (Honours) Flavia Howard BA (Honours) Jessica Johnson BA
Art Editors	Kate Sprawson BA (Honours) Keith Vollans LSIAD		
Deputy Editor	John Kirkwood B Sc (Honours)	**Production Controllers**	Steve Roberts Alan Stewart BSc
Sub-editors	Caroline Bugler BA (Honours), MA Sue Churchill BA (Honours) Alison Cole BA, M Phil Jenny Mohammadi Nigel Rodgers BA (Honours), MA Penny Smith Will Steeds BA (Honours), MA	**Secretary**	Lynn Smail
		Publisher	Terry Waters Grad IOP
		Editorial Director	Maggi McCormick
		Production Executive	Robert Paulley B Sc
		Consultant and Authenticator	Sharon Fermor BA (Honours) Lecturer in the Extra-Mural Department of London University and Lecturer in Art History at Sussex University
Designers	Stuart John Julie Stanniland		

Reference Edition Published 1987

Published by Marshall Cavendish Corporation
147 West Merrick Road
Freeport, Long Island
N.Y. 11520

Typeset by Litho Link Ltd., Welshpool
Printed and Bound in Singapore by
Koon Wah Printing Pte Ltd.

Library of Congress Cataloging-in-Publication Data

Main entry under title:

Great Artists of the Western World.

Includes index.
1. Artists – Biography. I. Marshall Cavendish Corporation
N40.G77 1987   709'.2'2 [B]   86–23863
ISBN 0–86307–743–9

ISBN 0–86307–743–9 (set)
ISBN 0–86307–752–8 (vol)

Preface

Looking at pictures can be one of the greatest pleasures that life has to offer. Note, however, those two words 'can be'; all too many of us remember all too clearly those grim afternoons of childhood when we were dragged, bored to tears and complaining bitterly, through room after room of Italian primitives by well-meaning relations or tight-lipped teachers. It was enough to put one off pictures for life – which, for some of us, was exactly what it did.

For if gallery-going is to be the fun it should be, certain conditions must be fulfilled. First, the pictures we are to see must be good pictures. Not necessarily great pictures – even a few of these can be daunting, while too many at a time may prove dangerously indigestible. But they must be well-painted, by good artists who know precisely both the effect they want to achieve and how best to achieve it. Second, we must limit ourselves as to quantity. Three rooms – four at the most – of the average gallery are more than enough for one day, and for best results we should always leave while we are still fresh, well before satiety sets in. Now I am well aware that this is a counsel of perfection: sometimes, in the case of a visiting exhibition or, perhaps, when we are in a foreign city with only a day to spare, we shall have no choice but to grit our teeth and stagger on to the end. But we shall not enjoy ourselves quite so much, nor will the pictures remain so long or so clearly in our memory.

The third condition is all-important: we must know something about the painters whose work we are looking at. And this is where this magnificent series of volumes – one of which you now hold in your hands – can make all the difference. No painting is an island: it must, if it is to be worth a moment's attention, express something of the personality of its painter. And that painter, however individual a genius, cannot but reflect the country, style and period, together with the views and attitudes of the people among whom he or she was born and bred. Even a superficial understanding of these things will illuminate a painting for us far better than any number of spotlights, and if in addition we have learnt something about the artist as a person – life and loves, character and beliefs, friends and patrons, and the places to which he or she travelled – the interest and pleasure that the work will give us will be multiplied a hundredfold.

Great Artists of the Western World will provide you with just such an insight into the life and work of some of the outstanding painters of Europe and America. The text is informative without ever becoming dry or academic, not limiting itself to the usual potted biographies but forever branching out into the contemporary world outside and beyond workshop or studio. The illustrations, in colour throughout, have been dispensed in almost reckless profusion. For those who, like me, revel in playing the Attribution Game – the object of which is to guess the painter of each picture before allowing one's eye to drop to the label – the little sections on 'Trademarks' are a particularly happy feature; but every aficionado will have particular preferences, and I doubt whether there is an art historian alive, however distinguished, who would not find some fascinating nugget of previously unknown information among the pages that follow.

This series, however, is not intended for art historians. It is designed for ordinary people like you and me – and for our older children – who are fully aware that the art galleries of the world constitute a virtually bottomless mine of potential enjoyment, and who are determined to extract as much benefit and advantage from it as they possibly can. All the volumes in this collection will enable us to do just that, expanding our knowledge not only of art itself but also of history, religion, mythology, philosophy, fashion, interior decoration, social customs and a thousand other subjects as well. So let us not simply leave them around, flipping idly through a few of their pages once in a while. Let us read them as they deserve to be read – and welcome a new dimension in our lives.

John Julius Norwich is a writer and broadcaster who has written histories of Venice and of Norman Sicily as well as several works on history, art and architecture. He has also made over twenty documentary films for television, including the recent **Treasure Houses of Britain** series which was widely acclaimed after repeated showings in the United States.

Lord Norwich is Chairman of the Venice in Peril Fund, and member of the Executive Committee of the British National Trust, an independently funded body established for the protection of places of historic interest and natural beauty.

John Julius Norwich

Contents

Introduction

The art of watercolour
(above) Although John Singer Sargent is best known as a portraitist, he was in fact more interested in landscape painting, and in watercolours like In a Levantine Port (c.1905-06), he displayed to the full his virtuosity in the portrayal of the effects of light.

The emergence of a fully autonomous school of painting in the United States took a surprisingly long time to achieve. Even before the Colonies had won their independence, America was producing artists of international stature, but these painters normally felt compelled to travel abroad in order to further their careers, and frequently never returned to their homeland.

The reasons for this were twofold: money and ambition. The young Republic could only provide a limited market for the aspiring artist, and that was largely confined to portraiture. 'Was it not for preserving the resemblance of particular persons', John Copley lamented, 'painting would not be known in the place.' In addition, Europe offered its wealth of artistic tradition; centuries of learning that would enable any student to cultivate and develop his talents to the full. Accordingly, a trip there was deemed a necessity by virtually every American painter until the end of the 19th century.

An American Aesthete

For James McNeill Whistler, Europe presented not only a source of opportunity, but also a means of escape. The puritanical influence of his family – who had thwarted his artistic inclinations and pushed him into his abortive military training – could not extend to Paris, where he settled in 1855. Whistler revelled in the bohemian existence he was able to lead in the French metropolis but, although he came into contact with artists like Courbet and Manet, his personal style did not truly develop until he moved to England.

He had travelled there in 1857 to see the exhibition of Spanish painting in Manchester and, while there, was able to appreciate the work of Pre-Raphaelite artists like Millais. These combined influences are evident in such masterpieces as The White Girl (p.24) and Miss Cecily Alexander.

Through the Pre-Raphaelites, Whistler also met the poet, Algernon Swinburne (see p.16), who was

The artists
(left, from the top) Edward Hopper at 42, in a self-portrait painted around 1925-30 after he had become a full-time artist; James McNeill Whistler in a self-portrait entitled Arrangement in Grey: Portrait of the Painter; *Mary Cassatt in a self-portrait; John Singer Sargent in a self-portrait of 1886.*

effectively the English spokesman for the 'art for art's sake' theories that derived from the writings of Théophile Gautier. These ideas, which were to form the basis of the Aesthetic movement, found their fullest expression in Whistler's lyrical views of the Thames (for example, pp.15 and 28).

Aestheticism was an offshoot of the Symbolist movement and, far from being an excuse for exhibitionism or effete self-indulgence, played a crucial role in the development of modern art. For, by denying the relevance of moral or intellectual criteria to art and by asserting that a painting's sole importance lay in the arrangement of forms and colours on the picture surface, the movement paved the way for abstract art.

The chief exponent of this style in England was Whistler's friend, Albert Moore, and the latter's series of serene classical figures (see p.20), arranged without meaning into rhythmical patterns, had a tremendous impact on the American. His ill-fated Six Projects (pp.30-31) were a direct attempt to mimic Moore, but using Japanese rather than Greek accessories.

One prominent feature of the Aesthetic style was the analogy made between painting and music, and Whistler fittingly entitled many of his pictures 'Nocturnes' or 'Symphonies'. In his famous Ten O'Clock Lecture – which could easily have served as a manifesto for the movement – he stated that nature contained the elements of all pictures, just as a keyboard contained the notes of all music, and that it was the artist's job to orchestrate these into the most glorious harmonies. Telling a painter to do nothing more than copy nature, he added, was like ordering a musician to sit on his piano.

The Reluctant Portraitist
By coincidence, Whistler's London studio later became the home of John Singer Sargent. Like Whistler, the latter came from a cosmopolitan background – he had visited Europe as a child – and also combined French and English influences in his style. There, however, the similarity ended.

Sargent's sober respectability could not have been further from the other's dandyism and Whistler, in a typically waspish comment, described him as 'a sepulchre of propriety'.

This propriety was, of course, a distinct asset in Sargent's career as a portraitist, enabling him to gain commissions at the highest level in society. By the end of the 1880s, these were forthcoming both in Europe and America, as the bravura technique, which he had developed under the direction of Carolus-Duran (p.77), helped him to rank alongside artists of the calibre of Anthony Van Dyck and Thomas Gainsborough.

However, like Gainsborough, Sargent considered his success as a portraitist to be a mixed blessing. In common with his English predecessor, he would dearly have loved to withdraw from portraiture and concentrate on his real interest: landscape painting. By 1908, when his reputation for portraiture was at its peak, he was refusing many commissions, declaring: 'No more portraits. I abhor and abjure them and hope never to do another, especially of the Upper Classes.'

Sargent's enthusiasm for landscape blossomed after his meeting with Monet in 1876, although he was given little chance to explore it fully until his move to England, a decade later. His experiments with plein-air painting were more conservative than those of the Impressionists but, particularly in his watercolours (see opposite), Sargent achieved a vivacity and freshness that, inevitably, were lacking in his highly finished portraits. His facility for sketching also paid handsome dividends with the much underrated work that he produced during his time as a war artist.

Sargent contributed to the introduction of Impressionism into England – the country where the style met with the sternest resistance – by co-founding the New English Art Club in 1886, as a venue where the latest advances of French art could be displayed. He tried to effect a similar conversion in the United States, but the greatest successes in this field were attained by Mary Cassatt.

Impressionism for America
Cassatt, like Whistler, saw Europe as an escape route from the restrictive influences at home and it was a measure of her early uncertainty that, when she began exhibiting in Paris, she did so as Mary Stevenson, using her middle name.

Cassatt's art is frequently compared to that of her mentor, Edgar Degas, and the two of them certainly shared many features in common. Both exhibited at the Salon and remained, rather circumspectly, at the fringes of the Impressionist group. For both, too, experiments with light effects and open-air painting were less important than an emphasis on line and gesture. The marvellously evocative rendering of the children's sprawling postures in pictures like The Blue Room (pp.58-9) and The Boating Party (pp.66-7) is ample demonstration of Cassatt's ability in these departments.

In contrast to other female Impressionists, Cassatt's range of subjects was disappointingly limited, but she compensated for this by her readiness to explore different media. The superb coloured etchings, which reflected her admiration for Japanese prints, are probably her finest works (pp.64 and 65). In addition, she played a vital role in communicating to her compatriots, the great achievements of the French avant-garde.

In part, this consisted of the practical advice she gave to Louisine Havemeyer, whose remarkable art collection is now in the Metropolitan Museum of Art, New York. More significantly, though, she saved the French dealer, Durand-Ruel, from bankruptcy and was instrumental in gaining for him the invitation to produce a major exhibition in New York, in 1886.

Two sisters
(below) Here in The Little Sisters (c.1885) Mary Cassatt demonstrates her sympathy with her subjects, as evinced in many of her studies of mothers and children.

The Portrayal of Alienation

This show marked the introduction into the United States of Impressionism and its success demonstrated that American receptiveness to modern artistic developments was beginning to outpace that of Europe. This trend was confirmed in 1913, when the Armory Show burst upon the scene, overturning established artistic values.

Edward Hopper sold a picture at the Armory – his first major sale – making it a landmark for him, as it was for so many other American painters. Admittedly, the exhibition did not stem the flow of artists travelling to Europe; however, it did produce home-grown responses to Modernism, such as Synchromism and Precisionism.

The Precisionist style, with its synthesis of Realist and Cubist elements, gave a firm indication of the strength of the figurative tradition in America and it was this vein which Hopper tapped so effectively. His own roots lay in the social realism of the Ashcan School (its leader, Robert Henri, had been his teacher), but Hopper soon eschewed their outward-looking attitudes to concentrate on his very personal vision.

In his mature work, Hopper came closest to Regionalist painters, such as Thomas Hart Benton and Grant Wood. Like them, he employed a clear, matter-of-fact manner, determinedly avoiding any stylistic flourishes and, also like them, he chose exclusively American material. However, the air of optimism and celebration that was so pervasive in Regionalist pictures was entirely missing in Hopper's canvases. In its place, he instilled an irretrievable sense of melancholy and loneliness.

Hopper excelled at the portrayal of alienation. His sitters were usually isolated, both physically and psychologically, from their fellow men and seemed pensive or withdrawn. This was accentuated by the gulf which the artist placed between them and the spectator. Thus, his figures might be glimpsed voyeuristically through windows or at curious, fly-on-the-wall angles (p.117). Where the spectator's presence was acknowledged (pp.128-9), it was with apprehension, as if the viewer were an intruder.

In this way, Hopper evolved a vision that was thoroughly American and yet also universal in its implications. His achievements signalled the arrival of a fully independent American tradition, ready – under the auspices of the New York School – to assume the leadership of the art world.

Whistler.
1834-1903

James McNeill Whistler was one of most original artists, and one of the most outrageously theatrical characters of the 19th century. Born in America, he spent much of his childhood in Russia before returning home to enrol as a military cadet. A failed chemistry exam cut short his army career, and at 21 he moved to Paris to paint. But it was in London, his home-base from 1859, that he gained fame – or rather notoriety.

Drawing inspiration from Japanese art, Whistler developed a daringly individual style of painting in which subject-matter was largely irrelevant, and harmonious composition all-important. To the Victorian eye, his pictures looked 'unfinished', and he even sued a critic for describing his work as 'a pot of paint flung in the public's face'. It was only late in his life that his art was appreciated. He died in London, aged 69.

An American Abroad

An ostentatious eccentric, Whistler was born in America but spent all of his adult life abroad. He viewed the world as a sophisticated, witty, and highly critical observer.

'To begin with,' wrote James Abbot McNeill Whistler in a fragment of autobiography he never completed, 'I am not an Englishman.' Although he lived in England longer than anywhere else, he was constantly travelling and always regarded himself as an outsider. He was born in Lowell, Massachusetts, but his father, Major George Washington Whistler, had resigned his army commission to make commercial use of his expertise as a civil engineer, and in 1843 he took his family to St Petersburg in Russia as the Tsar's engineer in charge of railway building. They lived in some style: the young Whistler skated on the River Neva, learnt French from his Swedish tutor, and developed a passion for military parades and firework displays.

OFFICER OR DANDY?

In 1845, when Whistler was 10 years old, he began to attend drawing lessons at the Imperial Academy and a year later emerged first in his class. But in the summer of 1848, his mother, fearing the effects of another Russian winter, took her family to London. In April the following year, her husband died of cholera and the family was forced to return

Robert Harding Picture Library

The aspiring artist
(right) Whistler arrived in Paris in November 1855, determined to become an artist. He immediately threw himself into the role of Bohemian dandy, roaming the streets of the Left Bank dressed in outlandish style. When the artist Fantin-Latour noticed him in the Louvre, he was so taken by this 'strange character in a bizarre hat' that he invited him to join his circle of artistic friends, which included the etcher Alphonse Legros and the painter Edouard Manet. Soon, Whistler joined Charles Gleyre's studio.

Poynter/Portrait of Whistler/Freer Gallery of Art, Washington DC

home to America.

Whistler's mother was an extremely pious woman, and it was her hope that her son would become a minister, but he had no vocation for it. A career in art was out of the question; so in 1851 he enrolled at the West Point Military Academy. However, he was not cut out for military life either: he rebelled against every aspect of discipline and when, three years later, he failed a chemistry examination, he was discharged.

By now Whistler was determined to become an artist and in 1855 he left for Paris. There he joined the studio of Charles Gleyre, who did not charge fees, and became an enthusiastic follower of Gustave Courbet, the Realist painter. He also set about perfecting his role as a dandy and wit. Physically, he was short and slight, almost dainty, but galvanized by restless energy. His hair, about which he was very vain all his life, was thick and curly, with a curious white streak at the front. His clothes were always eccentric: in Paris he favoured a broad-brimmed straw hat with a ribbon, a

A Russian childhood

(below) Although Whistler was born in America, he was raised in Russia, in the beautiful city of St Petersburg. Whistler's father was employed by Tsar Nicolas I and the family lived in considerable style.

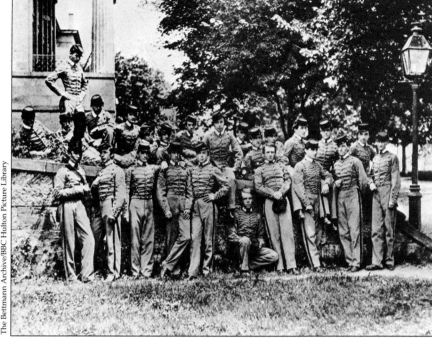

The Bettmann Archive/BBC Hulton Picture Library

A West Point cadet

(left) After his father's death, Whistler spent three years at West Point Military Academy. He was a terrible cadet – always chatting and laughing in ranks, changing ranks behind the sergeant's back and holding his bayonet incorrectly. In 1854, having accumulated an enormous number of demerit points, he failed a simple chemistry exam and was discharged.

Whistler's parents

(below) Whistler's mother, Anna Mathilda, was a puritanical woman, with a deeply reflective nature. His father, Major George Washington Whistler, had acquired a brilliant reputation as a civil engineer and was eager for his son to follow in his footsteps. He often warned Whistler not to let his taste in art become 'too poetical'.

monocle, a white suit, and patent-leather shoes. His manner was never less than theatrical, being a mixture of pugnacity and sharp humour.

In 1859 Whistler decided to go to London to live in the far greater comfort of his brother-in-law's house. He brought with him *At the Piano* (p.18), which in 1860 was accepted by the Royal Academy and praised by John Everett Millais, whom he greatly admired. By then, however, Whistler had quarrelled, not for the first or last time, with his brother-in-law, and had taken a studio of his own. He started work on what was to be his favourite subject for the rest of his life, the River Thames, making a series of etchings and a painting of the dockside at Wapping. He also began using the model who was to be his companion for the next seven years – Joanna Heffernan, known as Jo. She appears in his controversial early work *The White*

Glasgow University Library

Portrait of Major G.W. Whistler/Freer Gallery of Art, Washington DC

Key Dates

1834 born in Lowell, Massachusetts

1843 family moves to Russia

1848 lives in London

1851 enrols at West Point Military Academy

1855 decides to become an artist; arrives in Paris

1856 enters Charles Gleyre's studio

1860 begins affair with Jo Heffernan

1862 meets Swinburne

1865 paints with Courbet at Trouville

1866 visits Chile

1871 completes *The Painter's Mother*

1877 finishes the *Peacock Room*

1878 famous 'pot-of-paint' trial

1879 goes bankrupt

1881 meets Oscar Wilde

1885 delivers *Ten O'Clock Lecture*

1888 begins friendship with Mallarmé; marries Beatrix Godwin

1896 Beatrix dies

1900 seriously ill

1903 dies in London

Girl, and again in *The Little White Girl*.

After a holiday in France when he nearly drowned and had to be rescued by Jo, Whistler leased a house overlooking the Thames, near the old Battersea bridge. They lived there together until his mother came to England in 1863, and Jo was forced to remove herself to lodgings nearby. Whistler's mother settled into the house, but discreetly confined herself to the living quarters, never straying into the studio, except for once when she discovered the maid posing naked.

Whistler had now established himself as an artist of great originality and as one of the most extraordinary personalities of his times. He became acquainted with a wide circle of painters and writers in London, becoming especially friendly with Dante Gabriel Rossetti, with whom he shared a passion for collecting blue and white pottery and Japanese artifacts of every kind. But towards the end of 1865 he joined his original mentor Gustave Courbet at Trouville in France,

Tite Street, Chelsea
(below) From 1859, Whistler spent most of his time in London and in 1878, despite being heavily in debt, decided to have a house built for himself in fashionable Tite Street, Chelsea. 'The White House', as it was to be called, was duly designed by E. W. Godwin, the leading Aesthetic architect.

'Whistler versus Ruskin'

In July 1877, the famous critic John Ruskin launched an abusive attack on Whistler, denouncing the 'unfinished' appearance of his *Nocturne in Black and Gold; The Falling Rocket*: 'I have seen and heard much of Cockney impudence', he wrote, 'but never expected to hear a coxcomb ask 200 guineas for flinging a pot of paint in the face of the public.' In a fury, Whistler sued for libel, but although he won the verdict, he was awarded only one farthing in damages and never lived it down.

Punch cartoon
The court case caused great merriment in the press, but broke Ruskin emotionally and Whistler financially.

Nocturne in Black and Gold
(right) The painting at the centre of the trial was inspired by a firework display on the Thames.

and Courbet described him as his 'English pupil'.

In 1866 Whistler suddenly decided that his honour as a West Point man required him to see military action and so, pausing only to make a will leaving everything to Jo, he set sail for Valparaiso to help the Chileans who were then at war with Spain. He arrived in time to watch the Spanish fleet bombard the port and then hostilities were suspended. A prolonged wait ensued before he found a ship to take him home. The sole legacy of this farcical adventure was some fine seascapes and studies of the harbour.

Jo, meanwhile, had been driven by poverty to find work in Paris, where Courbet, long an admirer of the 'superb redhead', painted her in an erotic picture showing a pair of lesbian lovers. When Whistler returned to England, they resumed their old pattern of life, but only briefly. By the next year Jo had disappeared and was seldom mentioned by Whistler again.

Artistically, he was now very confused, and in his dealings with people he became incredibly intolerant. Inevitably, one of his victims was his

John Heseltine
BBC Hulton Picture Library

Nocturne in Black and Gold: The Falling Rocket/Detroit Institute of Arts

Harmony in Red: Lamplight/Hunterian Art Gallery, Glasgow

brother-in-law, whom he pushed through a plate glass window. Gradually, however, he managed to bring order back to his life and work. He vented some of his aggression by taking boxing lessons from a professional, and he began to paint his famous *Nocturnes* and portraits. Though the *Nocturnes* remained largely unsold, Whistler himself was confident that in them he had at last fulfilled his genius. The portraits were more successful, and for the first time in his adult life, Whistler got out of serious debt.

A NEW MISTRESS

In 1875, his mother, now 71 years old, was ordered to leave London for the sake of her health and Whistler moved his new mistress, Maud Franklin, into the house. Her portraits show her as slim and elegant, with glorious auburn hair.

One of Whistler's patrons at this time was Frederick Leyland, an extremely wealthy Liverpool ship-owner. In 1876 Leyland arranged to have his London house in Kensington completely refurbished. Its show-piece was a Whistler picture and he invited the painter to give his opinion of the new décor. Whistler suggested a few modest alterations and Leyland departed for Liverpool, leaving Whistler a free hand and the use of his account at a shop selling gold leaf.

Whistler seized his opportunity and, working in a frenzy throughout the summer, covered the walls, woodwork, window shutters, panels even the ceiling, with a design of blue and gold peacocks. He then invited friends, journalists and other patrons to admire his masterpiece, and issued an explanatory broadsheet. When Leyland returned, he was furious that his home had been thrown open to the critics and paid Whistler only £1,000, instead of the 2,000 guineas demanded. Whistler replied by painting an unflattering portrait of him, and the relationship ended.

If the break with Leyland proved a major set-back it was soon to be followed by a greater disaster. In July 1877 the great critic, John Ruskin, denounced Whistler's *Nocturne in Black and Gold: The Falling Rocket* (above) and accused him of

'Trixie' Whistler
In August 1888, Whistler married Beatrix Godwin. His previous relationships with Jo and Maud – both stunning red-haired models – had been long-lasting but tempestuous. Beatrix, however, worshipped him, tolerated his tantrums and was a gifted artist herself. Their marriage was, by all accounts, an extremely happy one.

Whistler's Poet Friends

In the 1860s, Whistler met the poet Algernon Charles Swinburne, and was soon intoxicated by the passion and lyricism of his verse. The admiration was mutual, and in 1865 Swinburne wrote a poem to Whistler's *Little White Girl* (p.24). However, the friendship ended in 1888, when the sickly and excitable Swinburne wrote a scornful review of Whistler's *Ten O'Clock Lecture*. Now, another literary figure – the French Symbolist poet Stéphane Mallarmé – took Swinburne's place in the artist's affections. Mallarmé, who sympathized entirely with Whistler's artistic vision, translated the lecture into French and became a stimulating friend.

Fitzwilliam Museum, Cambridge

Swinburne (1837-1900)
(above) Swinburne was part of Rossetti's brilliant circle: this portrait was painted by Rossetti in 1861. He formed a very close friendship with Whistler – addressing the artist as 'mon père' and signing himself, respectfully, 'ton fils'.

Lauros-Giraudon/© DACS 1987

Blanche/Stéphane Mallarmé/Musée des Beaux Arts, Rouen

Mallarmé (1842-1898)
(left) Whistler was properly introduced to Mallarmé in the 1880s, when his friend Claude Monet arranged for them to meet over lunch. Mallarmé admitted that the artist had always made a 'très rare impression' on him.

Glasgow University Library

The Birnie-Philip family
(above) Whistler's wife Beatrix belonged to the Birnie-Philip family; in this photo she is shown seated third from the left, and Whistler stands looking fondly down at her. After Beatrix's death, Whistler was looked after by her younger sister, Rosalind, who inherited his entire estate in 1903. Several decades later, Rosalind presented a vast Whistler bequest to Glasgow University.

'flinging a pot of paint in the face of the public'. Whistler, who could never resist a fight, immediately sued for libel. When the case was tried a year later, Whistler won the verdict – but only one farthing in damages. The cost of the trial pushed him deep into debt, and in the meantime, his reputation had slumped.

Despite his desperate situation, Whistler was living very extravagantly. In 1878, he had had a house built for him, the White House in Tite Street, Chelsea, and had become very friendly with his architect, William Godwin and his wife, Beatrix. Bills and writs poured into his new address; he even owed £600 to his greengrocer, who refused to be paid in *Nocturnes*. Whistler, however, preserved a jaunty indifference, and did not hesitate to use the bailiffs as waiters at his famous breakfasts. But the inevitable came in May 1879, when he petitioned for bankruptcy, declaring debts of £4,500. Two days before the sale of his effects and the house, he gave a last breakfast and left for Venice to join Maud.

During the ensuing months of hardship and exile he was very dependent on Maud's support.

Birmingham Museums and Art Gallery

The public image
(left) This caricature by Max Beerbohm presents the popular image of Whistler – the outrageous dandy, sporting a monocle, giving evidence in court. Although a rather small man – Oscar Wilde described him as a 'miniature Mephistopheles' – Whistler was always a larger-than-life figure with a flair for self-publicity.

In Venice he concentrated on etching and, when he returned to London in 1880, he held an exhibition that helped to restore his tattered reputation. He was commissioned to paint more portraits and a second exhibition of his etchings was attended by the Prince and Princess of Wales. Appreciation and respect were at last coming his way. A small school of followers gathered around him, addressing him, at his insistence, as 'The Master'. Most remarkable of the 'Followers' was the writer and wit Oscar Wilde. He and Whistler amused themselves with barbed banter, much of it reproduced in the press, and for a while they were on very friendly terms.

WHISTLER IN LOVE

In 1886, while Maud was in France, Whistler began to see much more of Beatrix Godwin, or Trixie as he called her, who was by then amicably separated from her husband. Godwin died shortly afterwards and Trixie became a regular visitor to Whistler's studio. Maud brought things to a head by posing naked for a young Follower named William Stottard, and on 11 August 1888 Whistler and Trixie were married. Probably for the first time in his life, he was in love.

Marriage seems to have mellowed him, and though there were fresh quarrels there were also new honours and successes. In March 1891 his portrait of Thomas Carlyle was bought by the Corporation of Glasgow for 1000 guineas. This sale made a tremendous impact on the art world. Shortly afterwards the portrait of his mother was bought by the French government for the Louvre and he was made an Officer of the Légion

d'Honneur. A large retrospective exhibition of Whistler's work was held in 1892 and he began to attract the interest of collectors.

Whistler and Trixie now moved to Paris to live in a house specially decorated in his fastidious style. In January 1894 the first instalment of *Trilby* by George Du Maurier appeared in America. The novel, which was an instantaneous best-seller, contained thinly disguised portraits of Du Maurier's fellow students in Paris of the 1850s; Whistler was unflatteringly represented as 'the idle apprentice, the king of Bohemia'. He was enraged and instantly wanted to sue for libel, but was advised against it.

At the end of that year Trixie became ill and they returned to London – she was found to be suffering from cancer. Whistler wrote that her illness made his life 'one long anxiety and terror'. He struggled to work, but his fears for her life had become confused with doubts about his own creative powers. To relieve his frustration, he indulged in more petty litigation. Finally, after they had moved to a house on Hampstead Heath, Trixie died in May 1896. Whistler was devastated by grief, but gradually recovered. During his last years, he fought one more legal case, which after two trials he won.

He was now suffering from a circulatory illness, which made him almost always feel cold. In the winter of 1900 he went to North Africa for the sake of his health, which he declared had been ruined 'by living in the midst of English pictures'. He sold his house in France and mostly confined himself to a house he leased in Cheyne Walk, Chelsea. In 1903, having been ill for some time with pneumonia and heart disease, he died. It is said that among the few friends and relatives who attended the funeral Jo, now an elderly lady, was to be seen.

Trip to the Hague
(below) In the last years of his life, Whistler travelled constantly but in 1902, while on a trip to Holland, he was taken seriously ill. Confined to his hotel in the Hague, he wrote to the Morning Post *thanking them for his premature obituary. He died in July of the following year, shortly after his 69th birthday.*

In Search of Harmony

Throughout his life, Whistler continually shocked the public by painting pictures with purely aesthetic themes – his main concern was for a harmonious arrangement of pattern and colour.

As a man Whistler was flamboyant, aggressive and sardonic; as a painter, however, he was the opposite, for on canvas he was subtle, discreet and sensitive. The scope of his creativity was perhaps narrow, but he was nevertheless one of the 19th century's most original painters: and, to the English at least, one of the most shocking.

AN UNCONVENTIONAL TRAINING

Apart from his lessons at the Imperial Academy in St Petersburg, the only formal training he received as an artist was at West Point, where a facility for drawing was thought indispensable in a soldier, and at the Coastal Survey in Washington, where he was taught cartographic etching. By the time he reached Paris, he had already achieved that independence of mind and confidence in his own method which was to amaze – and irritate – the world throughout his life. During his student days, he appears to have learnt far more from his circle of French artist friends than from his

The Taft Museum, Cincinnati, Ohio

The Lange Leizen (1864)
The oriental influence in Whistler's painting was initially confined to the decorative and exotic qualities of Eastern artefacts. Here, a woman in a kimono sits amid a profusion of bric-à-brac, taking her name from the long figures on the blue-and-white china which she is painting.

Purple and Rose: The Lange Leizen of the Six Marks/John G. Johnson Collection, Philadelphia

At the Piano (1858-59)
(above) This intimate picture of the artist's sister and niece was well received when it was exhibited at the Royal Academy in 1860. Influenced by the Dutch Masters, it shows a subtle use of limited colour and an interest in the musical theme which later formed the basis for the titles of many of Whistler's paintings.

Valparaiso (1866)
This seascape resulted from Whistler's journey to Chile in 1866, and shows a new attention to colour and light. In the twilight, the ships of the Chilean fleet are reduced to shadowy forms against subtle gradations of colour – a theme which is developed in Nocturnes of the Thames and Chelsea.

18

Screen with Old Battersea Bridge (1872)

Whistler's artistic interests encompassed all aspects of interior design. The bold simplicity of the moon-lit view on this Japanese-style screen shows a complete assimilation of oriental composition.

Little Juniper Bud (1896)

(right) In the last 20 years of his life, Whistler painted many close-up portraits, often of young girls. His late sketchy style is evident in this unfinished picture – a haunting portrait of Lizzie Willis, his housekeeper's daughter.

Rotherhithe/British Museum, London

A master etcher

(above) Whistler was trained as an etcher, and returned to this medium at various stages throughout his life. Rotherhithe was the most ambitious of many early etchings of life on the River Thames, made while he lived in Wapping.

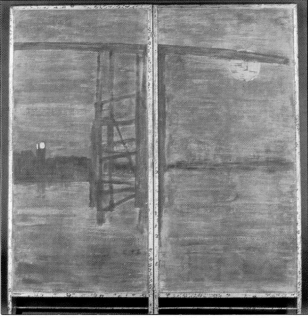

Blue and Silver: Screen with Old Battersea Bridge/Hunterian Art Gallery, Glasgow

Little Juniper Bud-Lizzie Willis/Hunterian Art Gallery, Glasgow

Crepuscule in Flesh Colour and Green: Valparaiso/The Tate Gallery, London

infrequent attendances at Gleyre's studio.

From the very start of his career Whistler was opposed to the kind of painting in which the English Academician excelled – namely the highly wrought genre picture, which either told a story or illustrated a conspicuous moral, using an abundance of anecdotal detail and creating a dazzling illusion of three-dimensional depth.

Whistler was not interested in performing tricks with perspective, nor in painting likenesses of familiar objects and places. He was solely concerned with what was to be seen on the surface of the canvas, with colour harmony, the play of light and shade, and the patterns made by shapes on the picture plane. He was reaching towards the kind of art we now call 'abstract'.

In order to stress the purely aesthetic intention behind his work, he often chose titles based on musical terms. Thus, his river scenes were 'Nocturnes', his portraits, especially of women, were 'Symphonies' or 'Harmonies', and portraits dominated by black and grey were usually 'Arrangements'. When giving titles to his portraits, he almost always gave precedence to the colour scheme over the name of the subject.

Whistler was by no means alone in drawing parallels between painting and music, but although he rather relished the annoyance his musical titles caused, he also used them as a declaration of his artistic creed. 'As music is the

COMPARISONS
Colour Harmonies

Just as a composer selects a certain key to create a particular mood in a piece of music, so an artist can choose a predominant colour to give a painting a distinctive atmosphere. Whistler stressed the importance of colour in the titles of his pictures, but other contemporary artists – such as Edward Burne-Jones and Albert Moore – also made use of resonant colour themes in their paintings.

Whistler knew both these artists well, and all three shared a concern for mood and aesthetic beauty, which they often expressed in terms of listless, beautiful women draped in dresses of a single colour.

Albert Moore (1841-93) Dreamers
A row of dreaming girls, dressed in delicate yellow and white are arranged rhythmically along a pale sofa. Though an oriental influence is evident in the fan on the right, Moore's decoratively elegant women were inspired by Greek sculpture.

Birmingham Museums and Art Gallery

Sir Edward Burne-Jones (1833-98) The Garden of Hesperides
(left) These mythical maidens, dressed in flowing russet-coloured robes, were the 'daughters of the evening' who guarded the tree's golden apples. Their dream-like expressions, and the autumnal colouring of their dresses, evoke the twilight world to which they belong.

Private Collection/Bridgeman Art Library

Whistler on Art

'Art should be independent of all clap-trap – should stand alone, and appeal to the artistic sense of eye or ear, without confounding this with emotions entirely foreign to it, as devotion, pity, love, patriotism and the like. All these have no kind of concern with it, and that is why I insist on calling my works "arrangements" and "harmonies".'

poetry of sound,' he once said, 'so is painting the poetry of sight, and the subject matter has nothing to do with harmony of sound or colour.' In other words, art is primarily a visual experience, not to be confused with literary or moral issues.

In his opinion, a painting was not truly completed until every trace of the work that had gone into making it had disappeared. The finished picture was to be a perfect representation of the vision originally composed in the artist's mind. This desire for flawless perfection made his method of painting extremely laborious and he often despaired of making a living because his output was so slow.

PAINS WITH PORTRAITURE

Nothing came easily to him, but he struggled most over his portraits. He took enormous pains over the preparation of his palette and canvas, the posing of the sitter and the arrangement of any props or draperies. Having made two chalk marks on the canvas to indicate the highest and lowest points of the figure, he would take up a large brush with a handle two or even three feet in length, step right back and make his first, sweeping strokes. Within an hour or so the broad outline of the portrait would be visible and he would begin the painstaking, and often interminable, business of filling in the details. His brushes would become shorter, his strokes lighter, and the intervals between touches longer and longer.

To the frustration of his sitters, on whom he had no mercy, he would frequently rub out the entire effort of a gruelling day. It is said that he began hundreds of portraits but in fact he finished very few. He was partly hampered by having little natural skill for drawing the figure, particularly men's legs, but he was also defeated by his ambitious concept of the portrait, which was to deploy the human figure as a motif in a more or less abstract composition. However, in the case of his most famous Arrangement, that of his mother, design and psychology are beautifully blended in a simplicity of line, colour and facial expression.

In his Nocturnes he met with fewer difficulties, though the process of painting was hardly less toilsome. By painting the river and the city at night or in twilight he was able to reduce the wharves and warehouses, boats and bridges, and even the

Butterfly Signatures

1873 1883

1894 1898

Whistler derived his distinctive butterfly monogram from the initials 'JW'. He began using it around 1870, and modified it at intervals. Later versions became unrecognizable.

Variations in Flesh Colour and Green: The Balcony (1865)
(right and detail below) This lovely painting was inspired by Japanese prints. The late addition of the butterflies increases its decorative quality, and – like the flowers set against an unshaded blue ground – emphasizes the painting's flat surface.

Freer Gallery of Art, Washington D.C.

people to simple patches of colour. These could then be arranged to fulfil their part in a purely pictorial design. As he said himself of his *Nocturne in Grey and Gold: Chelsea Snow* (1878), 'I care nothing for the past, present or future of the black figure, placed there because the black was wanted at that spot. All that I know is that my combination of grey and gold is the basis of the picture.'

Before painting a Nocturne, he carefully mixed his colours, sometimes taking longer to get them exactly right than to execute the picture itself. He often diluted the paints so thinly they would run down the canvas. In order to hold his 'sauce' he used very absorbent canvases which allowed him to create the impression of veils of colour, through which his shapes could emerge or recede.

In later life, Whistler painted a series of much smaller landscapes and seascapes, which he composed rapidly and on the spot, in contrast with his habitual method. Painting sometimes on wooden panels, he not only attained a vigorous flexibility in his handling of paint, but introduced bright, glowing colours. In these spontaneous little works, he came closer than any other 19th century painter to anticipating the modern abstract.

Symphony in White, No. 1: The White Girl

Whistler started painting *The White Girl* in December 1861, while he was living in Paris. The model was his mistress Joanna Heffernan, but the main subject of the painting is its subtle range of white colour. Rejected by the Royal Academy, it was first shown in London in 1862, and then at the Salon des Refusés the following year, where it caused a furore. In London the painting was seen as an attempt to illustrate Wilkie Collins' recent novel *The Woman in White*; in Paris it was interpreted as mourning lost innocence. But Whistler denounced such specific interpretations, and later prefixed the original title with *Symphony in White, No. 1*, making it the first of a series of paintings on this musical 'theme'. *Symphony in White, No. 2* followed in 1864, and *Symphony in White, No. 3* – a study of three figures – in 1867.

National Gallery of Art, Washington D.C.

A red-haired model
Joanna Heffernan's red hair provides a perfect contrast to the subtle tones of the background, as Whistler implied in an enthusiastic description of the painting: 'The picture', he wrote, 'barring the red hair, is one gorgeous mass of brilliant white'.

'Design is like the melody, colour the harmony'

Theophile Gautier 1856

Decorative frames
Whistler saw the frame as an important decorative element of his paintings. Here an incised basket-weave pattern is combined with a painted fish-scale design, which is signed with a butterfly.

Before the Mirror

Come snow, come wind or thunder,
High up in air,
I watch my face, and wonder
At my bright hair;
Nought else exalts or grieves
The rose at heart, that heaves
With love of her own leaves
                    and lips that pair.

She knows not love that kissed her
She knows not where.
Art thou the ghost, my sister,
White sister there,
Am I the ghost, who knows?
My hand, a fallen rose,
Lies snow-white on white snow,
                    and takes no care.

**Symphony in White, No. 2:
The Little White Girl**
This poem by Swinburne was inspired by The Little White Girl and attached to its frame when it was shown at the RA.

The Tate Gallery, London

Hunterian Art Gallery, Glasgow

Joanna Heffernan
(above) This etching by Whistler shows his mistress Jo, who modelled for all three 'Symphonies'.

Symphony in White, No. 3
(left) Whistler sent this sketch to Fantin-Latour while the painting was under way. He indicated the colours in French, stressing the pale tones.

The Witt Library, London

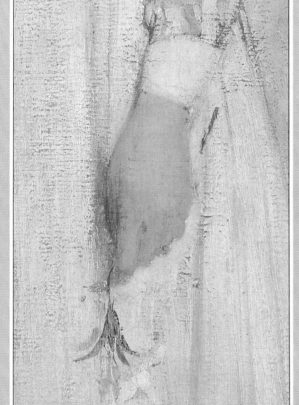

Shades of white
This detail shows the broken lily in the White Girl's hand – interpreted as a symbol of lost innocence. The flower, dress and cuff are all subtle variations of the colour white.

The bear-skin rug
(right) The tones and textures of the bear-skin rug, the blue of the carpet and the colour of the flowers all offset the white figure, while still harmonizing with the whole.

Gallery

Whistler's paintings can be divided into two main subjects – portraits and landscapes or seascapes – but as their titles imply, their real theme is harmony of colour and composition.

The White Girl marked the beginning of a series of full-length female figure paintings which also includes La Princesse du Pays. As Whistler developed his ideas on design

Symphony in White, No 1: The White Girl
1862
84½" × 42½"
National Gallery of Art, Washington, DC

This painting was the centre of attention at the Salon des Refusés in 1863, and was interpreted as a poetic fantasy. Simplicity of composition heightens the effect of the subtle colour harmonies which were, according to Whistler, the painting's true subject.

and colour, the decorative exoticism of these works gave way to the simplicity of the Painter's Mother. The light background, lack of detail and subtle range of tones set the style for later portraits such as Lady Meux and Théodore Duret. These are even simpler in composition and show Whistler's increasing mastery of a limited palette.

Whistler's preoccupation with colour harmony is particularly evident in his Nocturnes – the most controversial works of his career. Grey and Gold – Westminster Bridge, and Grey and Gold – Chelsea Snow are essentially spaces filled with exquisitely graded tones of light and shapes arranged on the flat canvas.

La Princesse du Pays de la Porcelaine *1863-4* 78¾″ × 45¾″ Freer Gallery of Art, Washington, DC

The title of the painting links the female figure with the oriental blue-and-white porcelain which Whistler collected so avidly. The work was bought by Frederick Leyland and inspired the famous Peacock Room which Whistler decorated for Leyland's house in Prince's Gate, London.

**Arrangement in Grey and Black:
Portrait of the Painter's Mother** *1871*
56¾″ × 64″ Musée d'Orsay, Paris

*This famous portrait of Whistler's mother was painted
while she was staying with him in London during the
summer of 1871. The figure is shown in profile, the body
flattened by the diffused lighting characteristic of
Whistler's portraits, and held in place by the lines of the
curtain, skirting board and picture frames. Whistler
later remarked: 'To me it is interesting as a picture of my
mother; but what can or ought the public to care about
the identity of the portrait? It must stand or fall on its
merits as an "arrangement".'*

Nocturne: Grey and Gold – Westminster Bridge c.1871-4
18½" × 24½" Burrell Collection, Glasgow

Like all his Nocturnes, Whistler painted this view of the River Thames from memory, simplifying the image to a pattern of essential shapes. The overall impression is one of space and harmonious colour, where the vast areas of water and sky are both broken and defined by dim silhouettes of buildings on the banks of the river.

Nocturne: Grey and Gold – Chelsea Snow 1876
18⅝″ × 24⅝″ Fogg Art Museum, Cambridge, Massachusetts

In this night scene, snow, buildings, trees and sky become abstract areas of light and dark, in a two-dimensional composition. The luminous snow and shadowy buildings are bridged by an anonymous figure – introduced because the design demanded a touch of black at that spot.

Pink and Grey: Three Figures *1879*
55″ × 73″ Tate Gallery, London

*This richly coloured painting is a copy of an earlier
picture commissioned by Frederick Leyland in 1867 –
one of the 'Six Projects' which made up Whistler's first
decorative scheme for his patron. Like the original, it was
never completed. The composition is heavily influenced
by Japanese prints, which Whistler collected along with
other Oriental artefacts. The work is one of the pictures
Whistler had in mind when he said his most ambitious
desire was to paint a grand concerto-like picture with the
title 'Full Palette'.*

Harmony in Pink and Grey: Portrait of Lady Meux *1881-2*
76¼" × 36⅝"
Frick Collection,
New York

The simplicity of this sensuous portrait and the subtle use of a range of tones show a new assurance in Whistler's painting. He began three portraits of Lady Meux, but only finished two. The third seems to have been abandoned after a disagreement in 1886, when she suggested his paintings were not properly finished.

**Arrangement in Flesh
Colour and Black:
Portrait of
Théodore Duret** *1883-4*
76⅛″ × 35¾″
Metropolitan
Museum of Art,
New York

*Whistler's fascination
with the contrast between
dark and light made a
figure in evening dress an
ideal subject, although he
found men particularly
difficult to paint. This
portrait of his friend, the
art critic Théodore Duret,
was repainted many
times: the head and legs
still show signs of
reworking.*

Art for Art's Sake

While Whistler explored the role of art and design in daily life, a self-conscious cult of beauty spread through Victorian society. Among the cultured 'aesthetes' was the legendary Oscar Wilde.

Whistler's insistence that his paintings should not tell a moral tale, but should be enjoyed for their own sake, made him one of the leading members of the Aesthetic Movement. In reality, however, there was no 'movement' and no members, only a social climate in which many people – from the Prince of Wales to the more enlightened members of the middle class – became aware of the importance of 'taste' in their daily lives.

For this cultured elite of the mid 19th century, art and beauty were to be enjoyed in every aspect of life, in the clothes they wore, the houses they lived in and the china they ate off, as well as in the paintings they admired. While the rich and famous might have an elegantly simple house designed by the architect Edward Godwin (as Whistler did), the less well-off could indulge their aesthetic sensibilities by buying a Japanese screen and oriental silks from the famous Liberty's store.

From 1875, Arthur Liberty's shop in Regent Street was the focal point of aesthetic taste in London. Crammed full of oriental objects –

Mansell Collection

Wilde as a sunflower
Oscar Wilde deliberately cultivated his image as the personification of Aestheticism. With his long hair, poetic demeanour and ever-present sunflower, he was an easy target for satire – especially since his poetry did not live up to his personality. A verse beneath this Punch *cartoon reads:*
'Aesthete of Aesthetes!
What's in a name?
The poet is WILDE,
But the poetry's tame'.

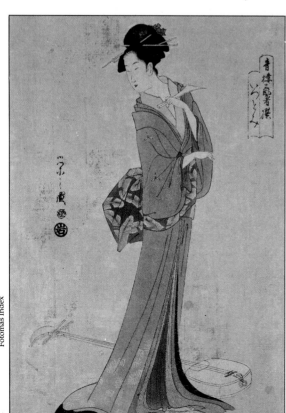

Fotomas Index

The cult of Japan
(left) In the 1870s and 80s, the fashion for Japanese decorative art became almost a mania. Japanism was synonymous with Aestheticism, and every aesthetic household boasted a Japanese fan.

A satirical opera
In 1881, Gilbert and Sullivan presented their comic opera Patience *which centred around a ridiculously camp young aesthete based in part on Oscar Wilde. The programme features blue-and-white china and sun-flowers: both symbols of Aestheticism.*

Victoria and Albert Museum, London

carpets, fans, screens, china and fabrics – it was the popular haunt of baronets, and fashionable ladies – as well as artists like Whistler and Rossetti. The craze for Japanese artefacts, which began in England after the International Exhibition of 1862, became so great that Liberty had to import from China and Persia as well as Japan in order to satisfy the demand. He even persuaded English textile manufacturers to produce Eastern style fabrics.

THE ILLUSTRIOUS AESTHETE

The new aesthetic cult soon gained widespread publicity. Just three years after Liberty opened his shop, a young Irishman arrived in London and deliberately exploited its appeal as a means of getting noticed. This was Oscar Wilde, who came down from Oxford in 1878 determined to make a name for himself. 'I'll be a poet, a writer, a dramatist. Somehow or other I'll be famous, and if not famous, I'll be notorious,' he declared. But although Wilde had won the Newdigate Prize for poetry at Oxford, in London his work was viewed as slight and derivative. To win the celebrity status that he craved, Oscar carefully manufactured his image as the most conspicuous aesthete of the day.

He wore his hair long; dressed in velvet coats with soft silk shirts and long flowing ties; and carried about with him the emblems of the Aesthetic Movement – sunflowers and lilies. And he mingled with the 'beautiful people', whom he dazzled with his wit and charm.

But the self-conscious nature of Wilde's public image made him a natural target for satire. George du Maurier, the caricaturist of *Punch*, had been satirizing Aesthetic tendencies since the early 1870s, and Oscar was soon lampooned – and easily identifiable – as the grandiose poet Postlethwaite. Then, in 1881, Gilbert and Sullivan presented a new comic opera entitled *Patience*, featuring a 'perfectly precious' young aesthete called Bunthorne – an amalgam of the artist Rossetti, the poet Swinburne and, of course, Oscar Wilde.

As one of Bunthorne's inspirers, Wilde was asked by the American promoter to make a 'personal appearance' lecture tour of the United

Aesthetic excess
(above and above right)
My Aesthetic Love *was one of numerous songs which mocked the vogue for aestheticism. The lady sits contemplating a lily surrounded by her aesthetic paraphernalia. The 'fop' teapot purports to illustrate the dire consequences of 'living up to one's teapot' – an 'in' joke directed against aesthetic pretensions.*

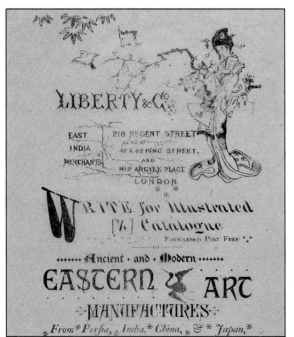

Liberty's of London
(left) As soon as Arthur Liberty opened his shop in 1875, fashionable customers flocked there to buy their oriental knick-knacks and fabrics.

Oriental textiles

(below) Soft Eastern material, dyed in pale hues known as 'Liberty colours', or with oriental designs like this cherry blossom fabric, were all the rage in the 1870s and 80s.

The Peacock Room

The peacock motif was one of the most pervasive aesthetic symbols. Whistler created the Peacock Room (detail, right) at vast expense; for the less well-off a few feathers would suffice.

Victoria and Albert Museum, London

Harmony in Blue and Gold/The Peacock Room

Freer Gallery, Washington

Walter Crane's Aladdin

(below) Aesthetic awareness extended even into the realm of the nursery. Before the mid-19th century, children's literature had only a minimum of illustration, but aesthetic parents were concerned that their children should benefit from tasteful visual experiences. Walter Crane's Shilling Toy Books, *with their delightful, Japanese-inspired designs were among the most popular story books of the period.*

States and Canada, to introduce transatlantic audiences to the ideas that would be satirized in *Patience*. Wilde leapt at this somewhat backhanded compliment, for he was always short of money, and was confident that he could subvert the idea behind the lecture tour to his own ends. In the event, Wilde overcame initial ridicule and scored a tremendous personal success as the apostle of Aestheticism. His audiences loved him, and instead of simply laughing at *Patience*, the opera's audiences admired the Liberty costumes.

Wilde and Whistler had become friends in 1881. They had acquaintances in common, they both lived in Tite Street, Chelsea, and they had a certain solidarity in the face of hostility from *Punch*. And when Wilde married Constance Lloyd in 1884, Whistler's talents were enlisted to design a suitably beautiful interior for the Wilde family home. Accordingly, an ordinary Victorian terraced house was aestheticized, eventually boasting a dining room done up in white, blue and yellow, and a drawing room featuring white peacock feathers let into the ceiling. Constance Wilde was soon known as the 'Chatelaine of the House Beautiful' and she and her husband presided over an elaborate series of receptions, with guests such as Arthur Balfour, Sarah Bernhardt, Mark Twain, and Lily Langtry.

Oscar also held a 'midday court' at the

British Library, London/Bridgeman Art Library

Oscar Wilde and the Café Royal set
The Café Royal in London's Piccadilly was a fashionable meeting-place for artists, musicians, writers and wits. Whistler was a frequent customer, and in his hey-day Oscar Wilde (left) held a regular lunchtime salon there. His guests included George Bernard Shaw, and Aubrey Beardsley – as well as his constant companion 'Bosie'.

Charles Ginner/The Cafe Royal/Tate Gallery, London

fashionable Café Royal, in London's Piccadilly. Whistler frequently attended, though his attitude to Wilde was sceptical. And it was at one of the lunch-time gatherings that the most famous Wilde-Whistler exchange occurred. After a particularly witty remark by Whistler, Oscar said, 'I wish I had said that'. To which came Whistler's acid response, 'You will, Oscar, you will.' The remark was said in earnest.

CONFUSED THEORIES

As a committed artist, Whistler had become increasingly galled by Wilde's opportunism. He saw him as the mere disseminator of an extremely diluted – and sometimes confused – version of his own ideas. And it irritated him that it had become fashionable to own 'art' furniture and peacock feathers, and to listen to Oscar Wilde.

In several respects Whistler's hostility was justified, for Wilde – the would-be-great literary figure – was still only a personality with pretensions. As yet he had written none of his great plays and when his only novel *The Picture of Dorian Gray* was published in 1890, it was severely criticized for its decadence and alleged immorality. And soon, such criticisms were to be levelled against Wilde himself.

Though he had two sons by his wife, Wilde had always been more involved sexually and emotionally with men. In 1891, he began an ill-fated love affair with Lord Alfred Douglas, the son of the Marquess of Queensberry. He was totally infatuated with 'Bosie' and flouted public opinion by appearing everywhere in his company. When Bosie's eccentric and violent father took exception to the relationship, Wilde made the great mistake of prosecuting the 'mad marquess' for libel.

Wilde probably thought he could take the offensive, because of his strength as the leading comic playwright of the day – all London now flocked to his plays. But his case against Queensberry backfired and he was bankrupted, then put on trial for homosexual offences. In May 1895 he was found guilty and sentenced to two years' imprisonment with hard labour. Upon his release he left England, and died in France in 1900.

To the Victorian eye, the fall of Wilde was inextricably linked with the decadent excesses of 'art for art's sake'. And though his trial had no direct bearings on the eclipse of the Aesthetic Movement, its date coincided with the opening of a new shop in Paris called *Art Nouveau* – the name of a new decorative style of art, which replaced Aestheticism and swept through Europe as the new century dawned.

A Year in the Life 1865

The bloody civil war that had raged in America for four years finally came to an end, but President Lincoln was assassinated only days before the final armistice. Times were more peaceful in Britain, but Queen Victoria too was obsessed with death, still grieving four years after the death of Prince Albert. As she withdrew from public life, the Prince of Wales caught the headlines.

Mary Evans Picture Library

The Pullman car
(right) The American industrialist George Mortimer Pullman introduced the railway sleeping carriage named after him – the Pullman car – in 1865. The carriages had upper and lower berths. The upper berths folded out from the wall, and the lower berths were made by extending the seat cushions.

Peter Newark's Western Americana

Peter Newark's Western Americana

Death of a president
(left) On 14 April, 1865, Abraham Lincoln was shot through the head as he watched a play called Our American Cousin *at Ford's Theatre in Washington. The assassin, John Wilkes Booth, a supporter of the Southern cause, escaped, but was killed 12 days later as he hid in a barn.*

A prince's memorial
(right) In 1865 Queen Victoria was still in mourning for her husband Prince Albert, who had died of typhoid in 1861. Of all the ways in which she honoured his memory, the most spectacular was the Albert Memorial in London's Kensington Gardens. Designed by the architect Sir George Gilbert Scott, the 175 feet high monument was built between 1863 and 1871.

Fire filled the headlines at the beginning of the year. Both the Theatre Royal in Edinburgh and the Royal Theatre at the Elephant and Castle in the south of London were burned down in January, to be followed a few weeks later by the Savoy Theatre in Sheffield. Then there was a serious fire at Marlborough House, the London residence of the Prince of Wales, and the newspapers were deeply impressed by the enthusiastic help given by the Prince to the fire brigades.

At one point the Prince led volunteers into the attics of the building in order to see whether the fire had taken hold in the roof. Unfortunately he did not realize that it was necessary to walk only on the joists, so he finished up with his feet sticking through the ceiling of the room below and had to be rescued from this rather undignified position.

Behind the scenes, dramatic confrontations were taking place. Lord Palmerston, the octogenarian Prime Minister, was quarrelling with his Chancellor of the Exchequer, Mr Gladstone, over the defence estimates. 'The morning went fast and wretchedly,' wrote Gladstone of a cabinet meeting at the end of January, 'the estimates settled at the dagger's point.'

QUEEN VICTORIA'S SPIRIT GUIDE

Palmerston told Gladstone that the only thing the country really cared about was keeping up its defences, especially against the hated French. Gladstone retorted that the Prime Minister himself, with his swashbuckling belligerence towards all foreigners, was trying to popularize an expensive defence

A sporting giant
Dr W.G. Grace, the most famous player in the history of cricket, made his first-class debut in 1865, playing at Lord's. He was 16 then and continued playing until he was in his 60s, scoring more than 50,000 runs.

Colin Molyneux/The Image Bank

Mansell Collection

policy which Britain neither needed nor wanted.

Queen Victoria shared Gladstone's distrust of Palmerston's chauvinism. Her beloved husband Prince Albert had had many brushes with Palmerston over foreign policy and now that Albert was dead she was determined that his views, the views of moderation and conciliation, should prevail over Palmerston's aggressive bluster. 'No human power will make me swerve from what he decided and wished,' she had declared at the time of Albert's death. 'His spirit will guide and inspire me!'

The devotees of the fashionable cult of spiritualism had taken her words quite literally and at the end of 1864 the *Spiritual Magazine* had reported that 'Her Majesty holds constant communion with the spirit of Prince Albert'. But the

Queen's morbid preoccupation with the dead and her almost complete withdrawal from public life were widely resented.

INTERNATIONAL UNDERSTANDING

It was left to the Prince of Wales to foster as best he could the spirit of international understanding which his father had cherished and for which Palmerston cared so little. One of the Princes's gestures in this direction was a visit in September 1865 to the Crystal Palace, London's most famous pleasure resort, in order to welcome a party of day trippers from France. The railway companies had laid on special boats and trains so that for a mere five francs – roughly five shillings in English money of the time – French visitors could leave Calais at four o'clock in

Tolstoy's great novel
The Russian writer, Count Leo Tolstoy, published the first part of his masterpiece, the novel War and Peace, *in 1865. The huge work, which centres on Napoleon's disastrous invasion of Russia in 1812, was completed in 1869.*

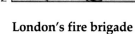

London's fire brigade
Fire insurance companies in Great Britain had had their own private fleets of fire-engines since 1772, but a series of disastrous fires in the 19th century showed the inadequacy of this system. In 1865 the Metropolitan Fire Brigade Act was passed and insurance companies handed over their facilities to a central Fire Brigade.

The South surrenders
On 9 April the Confederate general Robert E. Lee surrendered to the Union general Ulysses S. Grant at Appomattox Court House. This event is generally taken to mark the end of the American Civil War, but another Confederate general, Joseph E. Johnston, did not submit to the Unionists until 26 April.

the morning and return at eleven o'clock the same night.

English observers were a little shocked at the finery which French working-class women affected – 'bright shawls, ear-rings some inches long and remarkable petticoats'. And they were even more shocked at the way in which these members of the lower orders presumed to assess and criticize the statues and paintings on show. Whistler, who had spent the summer painting in Normandy, was rather less surprised.

Another of the Prince's public engagements was closer to the artist's heart. The River Thames, which was rapidly becoming Whistler's favourite subject, had been for centuries London's open sewer, into which all the filth of the city was regularly discharged. The stench from its waters was sometimes so unendurable that Members of Parliament tried to get their sittings adjourned in order to escape it. Now at last something was being done about this health hazard.

DEATH BY DROWNING

Joseph Bazalgette, engineer to the capital's Board of Works, was constructing a system of sewers which ran into two huge drains. These by-passed London, one to the south and one to the north; the 'Southern Outfall' was ceremonially opened by the Prince in April 1865. It was an impressive occasion, even though the works had already acquired an ugly reputation when 10 cadets from the *Worcester* training ship at Erith had been sucked down and drowned after rowing to visit them.

There was a General Election in July and Palmerston gained

The Salvation Army
In 1865, William Booth, a Methodist minister working in the East End of London, founded the first of his missionary stations to house and feed the poor. Booth gave his organization the name Salvation Army in 1878; it now operates in about 70 countries.

an increased majority. Gladstone on the other hand was thrown out as member for Oxford University, the staunchly Conservative constituency he had represented for 18 years. Instead he was returned as member for the much more radical constituency of South Lancashire. 'I am come among you unmuzzled,' he told Lancashire voters, thus leading them and the country to think he intended to challenge Palmerston's conservatism and press for reform.

THE END OF AN ERA

When the Bible fell from the hand of King James I's statue in Oxford on the very day of Gladstone's defeat, the superstitious saw an omen of coming changes. Palmerston, however, would not witness them – he died in October, leaving instructions that he was to be buried quietly in Romsey near his Hampshire home. His wishes were ignored and he was interred with great pomp in Westminster Abbey. The authorities claimed that it was the grandest funeral London had seen since the Duke of Wellington's in 1852, but at least one observer thought it was 'a most poor and mean business'.

The Times tipped Gladstone for Prime Minister, then changed its mind and suggested Lord John Russell instead. The Queen settled for Russell, but when Parliament met early in the new year it was quickly apparent that major reforms were on the way. Very soon 1865 was seen as the last year of the old regime – the death-bed of the easy-going aristocratic dominance that Palmerston had represented.

Archiv für Kunst und Geschichte, Berlin

Tristan and Isolde
Richard Wagner's opera Tristan und Isolde *was first performed on 10 June at the Munich Opera. Wagner wrote the libretto as well as the music, basing it on a Cornish legend.*

A great parliamentarian
(below) Lord Palmerston died on 18 October. One of Britain's most experienced politicians, he had held the posts of foreign minister or prime minister for more than 20 years and was noted for his belligerent foreign policy.

Spectrum Colour Library

A new capital for New Zealand
In 1865, the capital of the British colony of New Zealand was transferred from Auckland to Wellington – the city named after Britain's famous soldier and statesman.

Fotomas Index

Mary Cassatt: self-portrait/National Portrait Gallery, Smithsonian Institution

MARY CASSATT

1844-1926

The American painter Mary Cassatt left her native country to travel to Europe, where she studied the work of the Old Masters and came under the influence of the Impressionist painters Manet and Degas. Although she absorbed their style, she developed her own, highly distinctive subject-matter based on the intimate feminine world she observed in her own circle of family and close friends.

Throughout her career, the artist pursued the theme of the depiction of women in all phases of their lives, from childhood through to womanhood and maternity. At a time when women artists were frequently not taken seriously, Mary Cassatt achieved a great deal in obtaining recognition and acclaim for her work amongst connoisseurs and public alike by the sheer excellence of her technique and style.

'Give me France'

One of the greatest of American women artists, Mary Cassatt spent much of her life in France, where she found that she had greater freedom to pursue her chosen career.

The Legacy of Italy
(below) This early work –
A Bacchante – *shows the influence of Renaissance masters such as Correggio, whose work Mary Cassatt saw during her stay in Italy in 1872.*

The most famous female Impressionist painter, Mary Cassatt, was born on 22 May, 1844 in Allengheny, near Pittsburgh, Pennsylvania. The Cassatt family was affluent and cultured: Mary's father was a stockbroker, while her mother, who came from an old established Pennsylvania family, was an accomplished woman who spoke French and read widely, and provided Mary with an excellent example to follow. It is, perhaps, no accident that so many of the women in Mary Cassatt's paintings are engaged in simple, self-contained tasks like reading or sewing, since these were the everyday activities of the Cassatt household.

As a child, Mary travelled widely in Europe, since the family moved from Paris to Heidelberg and Darmstadt in search of a specialist who could help cure her brother Robbie's diseased knee joint, and to find the superior schooling that her brother Alexander needed for his future engineering career. This travel enabled Mary to learn both French and German while she was still young – linguistic skills that were to prove immensely useful in later life.

In 1861, when she was sixteen, Mary Cassatt decided to study art seriously and enrolled at the Pennsylvania Academy of Fine Arts, apparently against the wishes of her father, who thought it inadvisable that she should extend herself beyond the domestic role for which she was intended. She remained there for four years before moving back to Europe with her mother for a two-year stay just before the outbreak of the Franco-Prussian war. Henceforth, Mary was to spend most of her life in exile from her native country, reflecting a feeling among some women of her generation that Europe offered an escape from what they saw as the oppressive, patriarchal attitudes of America. She was later to say, 'After all, give me France. Women do not have to fight for recognition here if they do serious work. I suppose it is Mrs Potter Palmer's French blood which gives her organizing powers and determination that women should be someone and not something.'

On her return to Europe in 1872, Mary Cassatt went to Parma in Italy where she stayed for several months studying the paintings of the Italian masters Correggio and Parmagianino, and where

The Pennsylvania Academy of Fine Arts. Gift of John F. Lewis

Key Dates

1844 born Allegheny, Pennsylvania

1861 enrols at Pennsylvania Academy of Fine Arts

1874 meets Degas

1890 visits the Japanese exhibition at the Ecole des Beaux Arts

1891 first one-woman show

1895 buys the Château de Beaufresne

1912 trip to Egypt

1926 death in France

Portrait of the artist
(left) Degas painted this portrait of Mary Cassatt – which he named Melancholy – *shortly after he met the artist in 1874. It marked the beginning of a friendship that was to last until Degas' death in 1917.*

The Phillips Collection, Washington, DC

The Impressionists' Paris

(below) In the mid-19th century, Paris was the artistic centre of the world. In addition to the latest developments in painting, it offered a freedom to women artists that they often did not experience in their own countries.

she may also have studied graphic art with Carlo Raimondi. It says a great deal about the determination of the young artist that she was prepared to brave a somewhat lonely and isolated existence in order to achieve her aim. It is also significant that she should have felt a need to turn to these two particular painters, as they were both masters of the Madonna and Child theme, and subject paintings of women and children were to prove so crucial to her own work. From Parma, the artist went to Madrid, where she spent some time

absorbing the lessons of Velázquez in the Prado, and where she painted the Spanish-influenced *Torero and a Young Girl*. From Madrid, Mary went to Antwerp where she studied the art of Rubens for a time.

RELATIONSHIP WITH DEGAS

Back in Paris in 1874, Mary Cassatt established her studio with the intention of settling permanently in the city, and she began to submit her work on a regular basis to the Paris Salon. The early paintings show Mary's strict adherence to Realism, and bear witness to her professed admiration for the painters Courbet and Manet. Right from the beginning, she liked using subject matter drawn from contemporary life, rather than painting mythological or historical scenes. It was this quality of modernity, together with her directness of approach, that caused T. Edgar Degas to stop in front of one of Mary Cassatt's canvases one day in 1874 and exclaim, 'It's true. There is someone who feels as I do.'

For her part, Mary Cassatt had actually discovered Degas' paintings in the early 1870s in the windows of Durand-Ruel's gallery to which she had taken Louisine Elder, later Havemeyer, to buy a pastel. Not much is known about Mary Cassatt's relationship with Degas, as she burned all their correspondence before she died. However, it is generally assumed that the two were lovers, although nothing can be proved. What is certain is

The artist's sister
*(above) The Cassatts were
a close-knit family, and
the artist's mother, father
and sister came to live
with her shortly after she
moved to Paris. In 1880
they rented a villa at
Marly-le-Roi, near
Manet's house, where
Mary painted this portrait
of her sister, Lydia – who
died the following year –
crocheting in the garden.*

that the two painters had a close, if turbulent, relationship over a period of forty years that ended with Degas' death in 1917. Degas' difficult and cantankerous nature often led to periods of estrangement that could only be ended when mutual friends brought the two artists together again. It must have taken all Mary's reserves of diplomacy to deal with Degas' sometimes cruel nature. As she said in 1891, 'I have been half a dozen times on the point of asking Degas to come and see my work, but if he happens to be in the mood, he would demolish me so completely that I could never pick myself up in time to finish for the exhibition.' However, the two artists did manage to collaborate on a number of projects, including a journal that Degas planned to publish in 1879 to which Mary Cassatt and other artists of the time to contribute prints, and Degas also painted in the background to *The Blue Room* (p.58-9). These ventures undoubtedly helped cement their friendship, as they were brought together constantly.

It was Degas who persuaded Mary Cassatt to join the *Independents* – the exhibiting body that had been founded by the Impressionists – and the artist later recalled the event when she said, 'It was at

that moment that Degas persuaded me to send no more to the Salon and to exhibit with his friends in the group of Impressionists. I accepted with joy. At last I could work with complete independence without concerning myself with the eventual judgement of a jury. I already knew who were my true masters. I admired Manet, Courbet and Degas. I hated conventional art. I began to live.'

A FRENCH RESIDENT

Mary Cassatt also knew and befriended Manet. The two artists lived near each other, had mutual friends, and met from time to time. Although she and Manet do not seem to have had the intense and tortured relationship that she endured with Degas, Mary Cassatt knew him well, and in 1880 even spent the summer with her family at Marly-le-Roi near Manet's villa. She was also highly influenced by his art, and many of her early works show Manet's broad touch and his strong tonal contrasts. She was also responsible for sending many of his paintings to America.

The early years in Paris were a particularly happy time for Mary Cassatt, and this gaiety is reflected in the subject matter she chose for her

A Difficult Friendship

The Impressionist artist, Edgar Degas, became a lifelong friend of Mary Cassatt after first seeing her paintings in 1874, and acted as her artistic mentor and most severe critic. Degas had a difficult, pessimistic and cantankerous temperament, but Mary Cassatt's profound respect for his genius led her to preserve the friendship with great tact while maintaining her own pride and identity. The exact nature of their relationship remains mysterious, since Mary Cassatt burned all their correspondence before her death, but it is generally assumed that the two artists were lovers.

Sterling & Francine Clark Art Institute, Williamstown, Mass.

The young artist
(above) Degas' youthful self-portrait – painted four years after he took up painting – reflects his sensitive, melancholy and difficult nature.

Mary Cassatt in the Louvre
(right) Degas' etching shows Mary Cassatt perusing the paintings in the Louvre, with guidebook in hand.

W. P. Wilstach Collection

Philadelphia Museum of Art

Alexander Cassatt and his son Robert (detail)
(left) Mary's brother, Alexander, and his son, Robert, came to stay with her in Paris in 1884, when the artist took the opportunity to paint this portrait. She obviously had problems in persuading Robert to sit still, but Alexander did not mind posing as it gave him the opportunity to talk to his mother.

paintings. She depicted young girls sitting in the *loge* at the opera, women taking tea, knitting and reading. Many of her models were drawn from her close family and friends, such as her mother and her sister Lydia, who had moved to Paris to live with her in 1877. The charming picture of *Lydia Crocheting in the Garden at Marly* (opposite) is one example. It shows Mary's sister Lydia – who was to die only two years later – sitting in the garden of the villa at Marly-le-Roi, which the Cassatts had rented for the summer of 1880. It was also in that year that Mary Cassatt first began to paint pictures of mothers and children – probably because her nephews and nieces visited her then for the first time, and provided a stimulus to depict the relationship between mother and child that Mary, childless herself, knew only secondhand. On the whole, Mary Cassatt preferred to paint peasant women who took care of their own children, rather than the more affluent mothers who delegated the task to nannies or nursemaids.

In April, 1890, Mary Cassatt, in the company of Degas and Berthe Morisot, visited the exhibition of popular Japanese prints of the Ukiyo-e school at the Ecole des Beaux Arts in Paris. The prints were a revelation to her, as they celebrated the ordinary scenes of everyday life in Tokyo, which had an obvious relevance to the concerns of French painting in the 19th century, with its cult of urban modernity. The prints portrayed theatres, actors, domestic routines and mothers and children, all of which were of obvious interest to Mary Cassatt. They also stimulated her to set up her own printing press at the Chateau de Bachvilliers in the Oise Valley, which she rented in 1890, and where she set to work to produce her series of ten colour prints in the Japanese manner.

The following year, 1891, Mary Cassatt had her first one-woman show at the gallery of the Impressionist dealer Durand-Ruel. The year after, she was invited by Mrs Potter Palmer to paint the south tympanum in the Women's Building at the World's Columbian Exposition in Chicago – a commission she gladly accepted, as she had always been a champion of the feminist cause. Her chosen theme was 'Modern Woman', which she illustrated with a three-part composition. In the centre she showed 'Young Women Plucking the Fruits of Knowledge and Science', on the left-hand panel she showed 'Young Girls Pursuing Fame', and on the right she depicted the arts of music and dancing. The colours are cheerful, since it was felt that, as the painting was done for a national fête, the mood should be jubilant.

Young girl
(below) In the early years of the twentieth century Mary Cassatt turned to drawing pastels of brightly dressed young girls against plain backgrounds. This one shows a favourite model, Margot Lux, with a rather wistful expression and dressed in a big white bonnet and a rich amber dress.

Petit Palais, Paris/© ADAGP 1987/Bulloz

Japanese Prints

From the 1890s onwards, there was a growing awareness in Europe of Japanese prints, and in 1890 a major exhibition of prints of the Ukiyo-e School was held at the Ecole des Beaux Arts in Paris. The prints – which celebrated scenes of everyday life – were a revelation to artists in that they offered a solution to the 19th-century debate about the primacy between line and colour by giving each an equal emphasis. Manet, Degas and Monet used the prints as the basis for experiments in oil painting, while Toulouse-Lautrec incorporated their lessons into graphic art. And Mary Cassatt was also influenced, using large areas of flat colour, arabesque lines and acute angles of vision in both her paintings and her prints.

The Bridgeman Art Library

Victoria & Albert Museum, London

The winter of 1893-4 found Mary Cassatt in Antibes, recovering from the effort of producing her colour prints and the mural for Chicago. It was there that she began to paint one of her largest canvases, *The Boating Party* (p.66-7), which was highly influenced by Monet's painting *In the Boat*, which she had persuaded the Havemeyers to buy for their collection. At the end of the following

She had delayed her return home until this point partly because she was afraid of sea travel, and also because her ailing parents had needed her to stay with them in Paris. But after her mother died in 1898, there were no close family links to keep her in Europe, and she was free to visit her brothers Gardner and Alexander and their families in Philadelphia and Boston. While in America, Mary Cassatt decided to concentrate on pastels alone, as they were more portable than oils, and therefore more suitable for the journey home. Most of the subjects she painted there were women and children. Her attention was rather diverted from her own work when she returned to Europe; she made an extended visit to Italy with the Havemeyers to advise on the purchase of paintings, many of which can now be seen in American museums.

THE FINAL YEARS

The artist continued to produce a large number of paintings and pastels during the early years of this century, and she managed to preserve her general good health and strength until she was in her sixties. However, after a tragic trip to Egypt in 1912 during which her brother Gardner died, she found herself depressed, ill, and unable to work for almost two years. Her eyesight was gradually failing due to inoperable cataracts and because of this, the colours in her pastels became more strident and less subtle, although the artist considered them to be her best works. After a last outburst of work in 1913, Mary Cassatt stopped producing pictures almost entirely, and retired to the South of France during the First World War. She lived on in seclusion and virtual blindness, unable to work, until her death in 1926 at the Château de Beaufresne.

Gift of Paul J. Sachs, 1916

The Metropolitan Museum of Art, New York

Woman at her Mirror
(left) This print by the Japanese artist, Eizan, is typical of the intimate scenes of courtesans at their toilet that Western artists like Mary Cassatt found so appealing, and which influenced their work.

The Letter (1891)
(above) Mary Cassatt took up etching after seeing the Japanese exhibition. This is the fourth of a series of six prints executed 1890-91, and the oriental influence is clearly visible in the pose of the woman and her features.

year, Mary had her second one-woman show at the Galerie Durand-Ruel in Paris, and she bought the Château de Beaufresne at Mesnil-Theribus on the Oise, 27 miles from Paris, which was to be her summer home for the rest of her life.

It was not until 1898 that Mary Cassatt visited America for the first time since she had settled in Paris in 1874, in order to see her family and friends.

The elderly artist
(right) This photograph of Mary Cassatt was taken when she was in her seventies, sitting in her Chateau garden, and conveys the indomitable spirit of the artist.

American Impressionist

Mary Cassatt was much more than an excellent painter of women and children; she was also a superb printmaker, and her graphic work still influences artists.

Mary Cassatt painted a limited range of subjects, mostly restricted to women and children, and to housewives going about their daily activities, taking tea, sewing or reading. The world of her paintings is the entirely familiar, intimate, feminine one that she knew well, and on the few occasions that she actually painted grown men as opposed to male babies – for example in the portrait of her brother, *Robert Kelso Cassatt*

– they appear rather wooden and stilted in comparison with her women. In fact, the artist only painted a handful of portraits or figure studies of men. This was partly because social convention made it difficult for a woman to be alone in a studio with a male model except when the man was a close relative, and also because most women were denied access to the male nude, except in plaster casts found in museums and art galleries,

The Carnegie Museum of Art, Pittsburgh, PA. Patrons Art Fund 1922

The Nelson-Atkins Museum of Art, Kansas City, Missouri (Anonymous gift)

Lydia Leaning on her Arms Seated in a Loge (c.1879)
(left) Like Degas, Mary Cassatt enjoyed painting scenes of women at the opera and this portrait of her sister Lydia sitting in a loge resembles Degas' own portrait of the artist entitled Melancholy *(p.45). It was undertaken around 1879 when Mary Cassatt was beginning to experiment with pastels, and the brilliant colours – flaming oranges and sparkling yellows – reflect a new enchantment with the medium. The fascination was to last for the rest of her artistic career.*

whole, it can be seen as a portrayal of the various ages of woman, charting a progression from babyhood through childhood to maturity and old age. She began by showing an initial interest in children in her paintings of the late 1860s and early 1870s, and only later turned to modern figure paintings of women, and then once again to mothers and babies in the 1880s.

Underlying Mary Cassatt's work is a firm sense of draughtmanship derived ultimately from the

Kneeling in an Armchair (1904)

(left) This drypoint etching shows great economy in the means used to suggest the child turning awkwardly in her chair.

Emmie and her Child (1889)

(below) This painting is more sketchy than most of Mary Cassatt's work, reflecting the artist's experience of working in pastel.

Women Picking Fruit (1891)

(left) This painting is similar in theme to the mural of women plucking the fruits of knowledge and science that Mary Cassett painted for the Chicago Art Institute. It has the thinly laid-on paint and sharp contours that are so evident in the colour prints of 1890-91, and which are so appropriate to a large mural decoration. The intimations of a modern Garden of Eden link the painting to Symbolism.

and so had little knowledge of the male figure.

Mary Cassatt's women inhabit a self-contained world; they are perfectly self-absorbed and do not look out at the viewer. Perhaps the fact that they avert their gaze in this manner is an ironical comment on the whole spectacle of women observed. The artist is probably most famous for her paintings of women and children, and parallels have frequently been drawn between these and the Madonna and Child theme – one of the central motifs in Western painting. However, Mary Cassatt painted mothers and daughters just as frequently as she depicted mothers and sons, so the comparison is a general rather than a precise one. There are also important divergences from the convention in that the artist tended to paint straightforwardly naturalistic subjects that were not overloaded with symbolism. Of course, the artists she most admired were the Realists, and Courbet in particular, and their straightforward approach is certainly mirrored in her own art.

However, this is not to say that Mary Cassatt's work is without its own significance. Taken as a

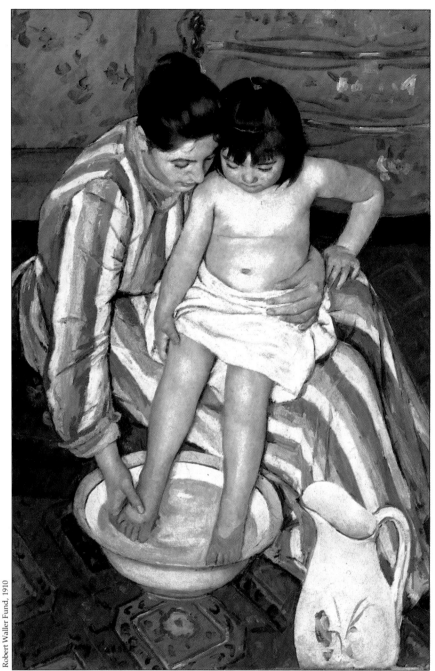

Courtesy of the Art Institute of Chicago. All Rights Reserved.

The Bath (detail)
(right) The two heads of mother and daughter are tenderly juxtapozed, and their expressions of rapt concentration direct the viewer's gaze downwards towards the mother's hand as she gently caresses the child's foot.

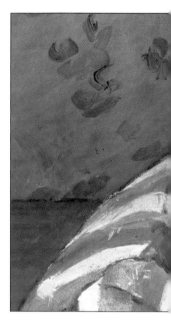

Degas, and the artist probably imitated Degas' method of blowing steam onto a pastel after sketching in the outlines, transforming the pastel into a paste, or sometimes blowing layers of fixative onto successive layers of pigment to make different colour combinations. This created depth and texture in her work, adding greatly to its suggestive qualities.

Mary Cassatt was also highly influenced by

The Bath (1892)
(above) This painting, executed the year after Mary Cassatt completed her first series of ten colour prints, clearly shows the influence of Japanese prints in its acute angle of vision, viewed from above, and use of space tilted sharply up towards the picture plane. The large areas of bold, flat colour also convey the Japanese influence, as do the oriental features of the little girl.

example of Degas, who is reputed to have said that he did not realize a woman could draw so well. Her forms seem palpable and solid; the outlines are always visible. Although the early Spanish-influenced paintings, following the example of Velázquez, have pronounced chiaroscuro contrasts, these are less obvious in the mature works, where the tonality is brighter and the colour is altogether on a higher key. Mary Cassatt painted her Impressionist works in broad, fluid brushstrokes rather than in the dots and dashes of colour used by several of her contemporaries. The pastels that she took up in the 1880s enabled her to add great luminosity to her work, and heralded an era of new technical exploration. In many ways, Mary new technical exploration. In many ways, Mary Cassatt's pastels resemble those of Manet and

Gestures of Tenderness

Although she herself was not a mother, Mary Cassatt had the ability to convey in her paintings a particular tenderness of gesture between mother and child. They are often shown embracing each other, or engaged in affectionate play.

Chris Vollans

Courtesy of the Art Institute of Chicago

Degas' compositional methods, his choice of unusual viewpoints, relaxed poses and natural attitudes. A perfect example of this is *The Blue Room* (p.58-9) on which Degas collaborated; the disposition of the furniture, the child's ungainly sprawl, and the use of perspective all suggest the child's viewpoint. Even before she had seen the Japanese print exhibition, Mary Cassatt had begun to compose pictures in areas of flat colour. In *Lady at a Tea Table* (p.62), for example, the picture planes are flattened, and pronounced linear contours are brought to the fore. The woman's features are lightly suggested rather than insistently modelled in a three-dimensional manner. This tendency to flatten was accentuated when the artist began to produce her own prints after seeing the 1890 Japanese exhibition.

The lessons that the artist learned from print-making were gradually transferred to her paintings, which became more two-dimensional, displaying large areas of bold colour. *The Boating Party* (p.66-7) with its vast expanse of blue water the navy sweater of the oarsman contrasting with the yellow of the boat, is a good example of this new style. This painting represents a general trend in Mary Cassatt's art that took place in the mid-1890s away from Impressionism towards more structured compositions, containing more solid areas of colour contrasted with pattern and solid draughtsmanship. Mary Cassatt's interest in the pure quality of line also led her to undertake drypoint etching, a medium in which no acid is used to bite the design into the plate, as the drawing is made directly with a steel or diamond needle. The prints involved a strange technique whereby softground etching was used in a revolutionary manner to achieve an unusual overall textured effect for the coloured areas. The invention of coloured etchings were a milestone in graphic art and Impressionist print-making, and one of Mary Cassatt's most significant contributions to the art of her time.

Mothers and Children

Images of mothers and children have been a central feature of Western painting since the Renaissance. They have their origin in the Christian theme of the Madonna and Child, but many women painters have taken the subject and given it a particularly personal slant by portraying themselves or close relatives with their children. The direct observations of maternity that women bring to bear on the theme often give it a particular impact, and Mary Cassatt's paintings share this mood of intimacy with those of the French 18th-century painter Elisabeth Vigee-Lebrun and fellow Impressionist Berthe Morisot.

Berthe Morisot (1841-95) **The Cradle** *(right) Berthe Morisot was, with Mary Cassatt, the most famous woman Impressionist painter, and a close friend of Manet. Her picture of her sister Edmee gazing with adoration at her new baby is a particularly moving example of the mother and child theme.*

Musée d'Orsay

Elisabeth Vigee-Lebrun (1755-1842) **Mme Vigee-Lebrun and her Daughter** *(left) This charming rendition of the mother and child theme shows the French 18th-century painter Elisabeth Vigee-Lebrun with her daughter, both dressed in classical robes in accordance with the prevailing fashion.*

Louvre, Paris

THE MAKING OF A MASTERPIECE

Lady at a Tea Table

This portrait of Mrs Riddle, a distant cousin of Mary Cassatt, was begun in 1883 and finished two years later. Mary Cassatt was very conscious of the difficulties involved in portraying a member of her family, and she wrote to her family: 'As they are not very artistic in their likes and dislikes of pictures and as a likeness is a hard thing to make to please the nearest friends, I don't know what the results will be. Annie ought to like it in one respect for both Degas and Raffaelli said it was "la distinction même".' But the picture did not appeal to the family, and the artist hid it for years until Mrs Havemeyer found it in 1914 and insisted on its being exhibited in the Metropolitan Museum.

American and Dutch influence
(right) This portrait contains echoes of Whistler's portrait of his mother (pp.26-7) in its stiff monumentality of pose, in its peculiarly static quality, and its use of blue to create a colour harmony. It also relates to Dutch genre paintings of the 17th century which both Cassatt and Whistler admired.

Gift of Mary Cassatt, 1923

The Metropolitan Museum of Art, New York

Drawing for 'Lydia and her Mother at Tea'
(left) Mary Cassatt treated the tea-drinking theme in several other pictures, including this drawing of her sister Lydia and her mother, which is a preparatory sketch for the softground and aquatint print Five O'Clock Tea. *There is also a painting of the same subject in which the composition is reversed.*

'a world of ease, but more

harmonious, more elegant'

J.-K. Huysmans 1880

Detail: Lady at a Tea Table

Blue and white

(above) *The still-life of blue and white china on the table in front of Mrs Riddle is one of the most notable features of the painting. It relates closely to Manet's work, in which such details also feature prominently. The Canton china tea service itself shows a continuing fascination with the East in Europe and America.*

The Cup of Tea (1879)

(right) *Four years before she began her picture of Mrs Riddle, Mary Cassatt painted this portrait of her sister, Lydia, drinking tea in her sitting room. The mood depicted here is intimate and casual, rather than stiff and formal as in the image of Mrs Riddle.*

From the Collection of James Stillman, Gift of Dr Ernest G. Stillman, 1922

The Metropolitan Museum of Art, New York

Detail: Lady at a Tea Table

A stern gaze

(left) *Mary Cassatt captured the tight-lipped expression of the elderly matron with great subtlety. Her impassivity and severe hairstyle carry echoes of the mother in Degas' painting* The Belleli Family.

Gallery

Cassatt first achieved public success with scenes in the then popular Spanish idiom, such as On the Balcony During a Carnival and Torero and Young Girl. Soon, however, she was drawn towards the work of the Impressionists and devoted herself mainly to everyday life scenes done in the light, fresh colours for which they are famous.

On the Balcony during the Carnival *1872*
393/4" × 321/2"
Philadelphia Museum
of Art

There was a great vogue for Spanish subjects in France at the time Cassatt painted this picture and the one on the opposite page. Manet was one of the leaders of the fashion and, like him, Cassatt herself visited Spain. This was the first of her pictures to be accepted by the Paris Salon; she exhibited it there under the name 'Mary Stevenson', perhaps because of family disapproval of her choice of career. The subject of figures on a balcony had been treated in well-known works by Goya (Metropolitan Museum, New York) and Manet (Musée d'Orsay, Paris), but in its lively and picturesque qualities Cassatt's painting is closer in spirit to the genre paintings of the 17th-century Spanish painter Murillo.

Most of Cassatt's paintings show only one or two figures, generally captured in some quiet and inconsequential activity, or sometimes, in effect, doing nothing (The Blue Room). However, her subtle handling of light and colour, and her undemonstrative but unerring sense of character, give to these intimate images a peculiar beauty of mood.

She preferred indoor scenes, but also painted memorable paintings in outdoor settings, such as The Boating Party.

Cassatt's skills with the tools of the printmaker were remarkable also. The delicate beauty of The Fitting and Woman Bathing shows why she is considered one of the greatest graphic artists of the 19th century.

Torero and Young Girl
1873
39¾″ × 33½″ Sterling and Francine Clark Art Institute, Williamstown, Massachusetts

In 1874 Cassatt showed this picture and On the Balcony during the Carnival *(opposite) at the National Academy of Design in New York, whose exhibitions had a prestige in America comparable to those of the Salon in France. This was the year of the first Impressionist exhibition in Paris, and Cassatt's picture, although lively in brushwork, differed from that of her radical contemporaries in its academic solidity of form and its fairly muted tonality. It must have taken great strength of purpose for a young woman, who was beginning to make a name for herself in the male-dominated art world, to risk ridicule by changing her style and aligning herself with the Impressionists, who were then often subject to mocking attacks.*

57

The Blue Room (Little Girl in a Blue Armchair) *1878*
35¼" × 51⅛"; Oil on canvas. National Gallery of Art, Washington, DC

Cassatt's move towards a more Impressionistic style is clearly seen in this painting, not only in the high-keyed colour and dashing brushwork, but also in the snapshot-like cropping at the edges of the picture, which helps to create its remarkable air of immediacy and informality. This kind of cropping is particularly associated with Degas, whom she met in 1877 and whose advice and encouragement meant much to her. Indeed, Degas actually took a hand in this picture – Cassatt wrote of his involvement: 'I had done the child in the armchair and he found it good and advised me on the background and even worked on it.'

Woman and Child Driving *1879*
35¾″ × 54″ Philadelphia Museum of Art

Mary Cassatt never painted pure landscape, but she did occasionally use the countryside as a setting for figure painting, as in this picture. The painting shows her sister Lydia, a niece of Degas called Odile Fièvre, and the Cassatt family's young groom driving through the Bois de Boulogne in a small carriage they had purchased that year. The severely cropped composition recalls works by Degas, in particular his **Carriage at the Races,** *which was shown at the First Impressionist Exhibition in 1874.*

Lady at a Tea Table *1883-5*
29⅜″ × 24½″ The Metropolitan Museum of Art, New York

This monumental image of one of the artist's distant relatives
demonstrates the diversity of her sources. The pyramidical form of the
dress, the severe hairstyle and the way in which the head breaks through
the picture frame refer to Degas' painting of the Belleli family, and there
are echoes of Whistler's portrait of his mother.

Susan on a Balcony Holding a Dog *1883*
39½″ × 25½″ Collection of The Corcoran Gallery of Art,
Washington, DC

*Susan, a woman who worked for the Cassatts, is seen here in a view
overlooking the rooftops of Paris – an unusual feature in a work by
Cassatt, who rarely portrayed the urban scene. This picture is one of
the finest examples of her mastery of light and texture – the
treatment of the dress is particularly memorable.*

63

The Fitting *1891*
14½″ × 10″ The Metropolitan Museum of Art, New York

Cassatt was one of the most original graphic artists of her period and was a technical virtuoso. This colour print and the one on the opposite page were made from plates on which she had used three different engraving methods – drypoint, softground etching and aquatint. The effect, however, seems spontaneous and not at all laboured.

Woman Bathing *1891*
14″ × 10¼″ The Metropolitan Museum of Art, New York

*Cassatt rarely equalled this print for boldness of conception and
vigour of line. The subject of a woman washing herself was one that
her mentor Degas treated many times, but the subtle colouring and
rhythmic vitality make this image inimitably Cassatt's own. The
sparse but beautifully judged forms are typical of her graphic work.*

The Boating Party *1893-4*
35½″ × 46⅛″ The National Gallery of Art, Washington, DC

Cassatt painted this picture at Antibes, a small town on the Mediterranean coast of France that was a popular resort with artists. The painting is often compared with a famous picture by Manet, Boating, 1874 (Metropolitan Museum, New York), a work that Cassatt knew well. They have in common the use of a very close viewpoint, great vigour of presentation and the use of the blue of the water to fill all (or almost all) the background. The two paintings differ greatly in atmosphere, however. Manet's has a captivating sense of breezy open-air enjoyment; Cassatt's is more psychologically involved, with the three figures linked by somewhat uneasy expressions. The complete unsentimentality of the portrayal of the child – in its awkward, sprawling pose – is typical of Mary Cassatt's work and contributes greatly to the way in which we feel we have been brought into intimate contact with a moment of everyday life.

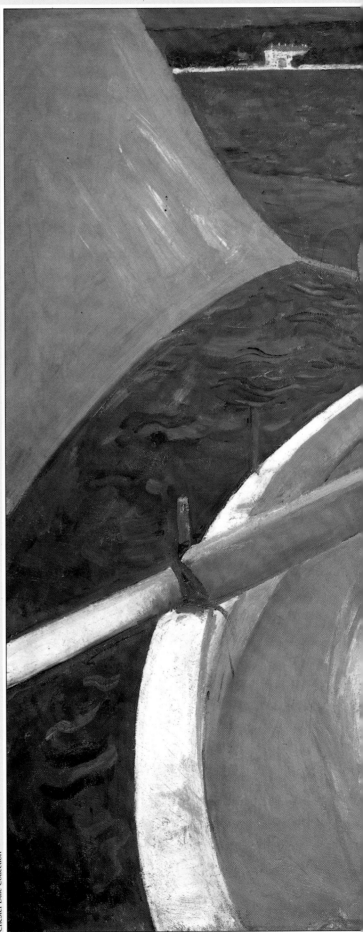

Chester Dale Collection

'A movable feast'

Le bar du Croûti

In the 1920s, Paris became the Promised City for many young Americans who discovered, like Mary Cassatt in the 1860s, that France gave them a freedom impossible at home.

'When good Americans die, they go to Paris', wrote Oscar Wilde in 1893. Thirty years later, Americans went to Paris not when they were dead, but when they were very much alive and *young*. For a delirious decade after the First World War until the Great Crash of 1929, fresh boatloads of Americans streamed across the Atlantic to congregate in a Paris that was their Promised City. Back home were Prohibition and the puritan ethic of work and responsibility. In Paris, young Americans could dance, drink and love.

CITY OF WRITERS

They also wrote. An extraordinary constellation of writers, poets (and a few painters) decided that 'Paris was where the 20th century was', in the words of Gertrude Stein, a trail-blazer and – to some – a sibyl. Ernest Hemingway, F. Scott Fitzgerald, Sylvia Beach, e. e. cummings, Hart Crane, John Glassco, Ezra Pound, John Dos Passos, Djuna Barnes, Harry Crosby – among

others whose names have proved less imperishable – lived for much of that notorious decade in Paris, making odd ventures to Spain, Provence or further afield, but always returning. For as Hemingway later put it, 'If you are lucky enough to have lived in Paris as a young man, then wherever you go for the rest of your life, it stays with you, for Paris is a movable feast.'

Before the War, Paris had not been the chosen city of American writers. Henry James, T. S. Eliot and Ezra Pound had settled in London, moving in English artistic and literary circles. Mary Cassatt had been exceptional in preferring Paris as early as the 1870s, but she was in many ways isolated from Americans abroad.

But in 1920 Ezra Pound left England for good, living for several crucial years in Paris as a mentor to and encourager of budding American writers. Paris held many obvious attractions for Americans: it was cheap (though not as cheap as Berlin or Vienna); Ezra Pound or Djuna Barnes could stalk around in long black capes or odd hats,

Café society
(below) The café Le Rotonde on Bastille day (14 July) 1925. With the Select and the Dôme, it was one of the Montparnasse cafés where many Americans in Paris met, to drink, to exchange news, views and gossip and to write.

Title illustration from Mary Evans Picture Library

Literary father figure
(right) Ezra Pound lived in Paris in the early 1920s, acting as literary godfather to half a generation of young writers, including Ernest Hemingway, T. S. Eliot and James Joyce, whose great novel Ulysses *was first published by Sylvia Beach.*

© Estate of Mrs G. A. Wyndham Lewis. By Permission.

P. Wyndham Lewis: Ezra Pound (1939)/Tate Gallery, London

Jean-Loup Charmet

that were the creating Modern Movement – Picasso, Modigliani, Stravinsky, Branscusi – joining French lumini such as Braque, Matisse, Gide and Cocteau.

America-in-Paris divided geographically and socially into two, mainly separate, communities. The Paris of rich Americans lay on the Right Bank, stretching from the Place de l'Etoile east to the Louvre. This was the Paris of the grand hotels like the Ritz or the Grillon, of the luxury shops and gilded restaurants, once frequented by Russian grand dukes and now overrun by young Americans fresh from Harvard or Princeton – or cotton millionaires from Egypt. But it was the Americans who set the tone. The Ritz bar became the centre of this Paris and was ruled by Americans making up for lost drinks at home. From these glittering establishments they set off on nightclub crawls – Zelli's was the most popular at the time – emerging at dawn to drink onion soup from stalls in the Les Halles markets . . . and all the time spending, spending, spending. This America-in-Paris popped and vanished in 1929, like a champagne bubble.

Across the river was a very different type of America-in-Paris: a colony of paupers and, sometimes, geniuses. Largely confined to the sixth *arrondissement*, its three great landmarks were the

Joie de vivre
(above) A nightclub in Montmartre in the 1920s. By then, Montmartre was no longer the artistic centre of Paris, but its nightlife was as dazzling, as wild and popular as ever.

risking no censurious glances; e. e. cummings or Scott Fitzgerald could drink all day in cafés, without fear of interruption by Prohibition agents or even English policemen (new restrictions on drinking hours had been introduced in England during the War); and sexual antics were viewed with an amused indulgence then only dreamed of in the Anglo-Saxon world. Above all, Paris had already attracted a swarm of Latin or Slavic artists

La belle Mistinguett
(above) One of the most famous of French cabaret artistes, Mistinguett epitomized the glamour and allure of Paris in the 1920s.

H. Roger-Viollet

American idol
(below) Ernest
Hemingway was one of
the most famous of
American writers in Paris
– a life he recalled in his
book, A Movable Feast,
30 years later.

**Shakespeare and
Company**
(right) This bookshop, run
by Sylvia Beach, offered
more than a mere shop to
penniless writers. Free
books, loans and meals
helped many.

UPI/Bettmann Newsphotos/BBC Hulton Picture Library

Patrick Heron: T. S. Eliot/The National Portrait Gallery, London

cafés on the Boulevard Montparnesse – the Dôme,
the Rotonde, the Select. The Dôme in particular
was where young writers headed when they first
arrived or returned to Paris. They went there to see
who was eating with whom, who had quarrelled
with whom, who was sleeping with whom and
who had just got published by whom. For several
American publishers used to go there to inquire
about young authors. Hemingway, who in 1923
still dropped into the Dôme for his morning coffee
(later he came to prefer the quiet Closèrie des Lilas,
where he could write without being surrounded
by would-be artists), would offer round the
manuscripts of his short stories for comment. They
got very mixed receptions at the time, though
Hemingway became the idol of many after the
publication of *The Sun Also Rises* in 1926.

Another, less frenetic, meeting place was
Shakespeare and Company, the legendary
bookshop run by Sylvia Beach at 12 Rue de
l'Odeon. This was far more than a bookshop, for
Sylvia Beach offered not only books – often free to
indigent young writers like Hemingway – but also
advice, introductions and even a printing press. To
Sylvia Beach goes the distinction of having

published in 1922 the first edition of *Ulysses* by
James Joyce – whose genius stunned many young
American writers.

Harry Crosby, another American in Paris,
established the Black Sun Press which published
editions of works by Hart Crane, Ezra Pound,
D. H. Lawrence and James Joyce. The Press had

The Waste Land
(above) T. S. Eliot took the
manuscript of his great
poem The Waste Land
to Paris for Pound's
comments – all roads led
to Paris then.

Edimedia

An American in Paris

(left) George Gershwin's music provided both the background music and the inspiration for the film of the same name. This, although it was made in 1950, tried to recapture the light-hearted and romantic spirit of the many young Americans who gave Paris its carnival atmosphere in the 1920s – at least for the rich. For poor writers, life could be much tougher.

been founded in 1927, originally to publish Crosby's own sun-and-death-obsessed poems. Crosby, far more than Fitzgerald, united the two worlds of American Paris. Coming from a patrician and very wealthy Boston family, he had fought in France during World War One, winning the Croix de Guerre – 'Oh Boy!!!!!!!' he had noted ecstatically in his diary. Returning to America, he found Harvard, and the banker's life destined for him, unbearably tame and moved to Paris with his wife, Caresse (whose original name was Mary).

THE END OF THE DREAM

The Crosbys' wild life was perhaps epitomized by the Four Arts Ball, stage every June by art students. The ball was attended by up to 3,000 men and women – the latter students or prostitutes if French, prominent ladies slumming it if American or British – and each year there was a different theme for the costumes. In 1926 it was Incan. Crosby painted himself red and gave a supper party beforehand with a punch made of 40 bottles of champagne plus one each of whisky, cointreau and gin. Caresse Crosby had bare breasts and a turquoise wig, and at the ball won a prize by riding around the ballroom in the jaws of papier maché dragon propelled by a dozen drunk students. Then the Crosbys entertained many people in their own bed, all sticky with paint. And Crosby considered himself a serious man.

In November 1929 Crosby shot himself – along with his mistress of the moment – in a New York hotel bedroom. This most aptly punctuated the end of the decade. Within months, with the Wall Street Crash in October, the Americans had returned or dispersed; the movable feast was over.

In the end, as in the beginning, Gertrude Stein, sober and sardonic, was left with Alice B. Toklas and her dogs, because, as she said, her generation felt the way about Paris that the Victorian English had felt about Italy – that it was *the* other country.

Portrait in a red checkered sweater

Rhapsody in Paris

(left) George Gershwin, the New York composer, wrote the music, An American in Paris, *which best captured the spirit of young Americans in Paris, with its jazzy rhythms and mingling high spirits and melancholy. Gershwin was only 30 when he composed the work in 1928 – suitably youthful for the age of youth.*

From *The Gershwins* by Robert Kimball and Alfred Simon

A Year in the Life 1878

By 1878, Mary Cassatt had settled in Paris with her mother and sister and, at the invitation of Edgar Degas, had become a member of the *Independents* group of Impressionist painters. In the wider world, however, the times were overshadowed by the threat of war among the Great Powers.

The Exposition that opened in 1878 at the wildly ornate Troeadero Palace in Paris was to leave no lasting monument to compare with the Eiffel Tower, erected for the 1889 Exposition. The palace itself – described by one critic as 'an enormous architectural braggart' – was replaced by the present austere structure in 1936. Yet the Exposition signalled both to the French nation and to the rest of the world the rebirth of Paris. Put aside were the events of the previous eight years: the crushing defeat by Germany in 1870, followed by the four-month siege of the capital itself; then the violent and violently suppressed rising of the Communards, and finally the humiliation of having the Germans march in triumph through the Arc de Triomphe, while an impotent government dithered and cowered in Versailles. Paris was once more the City of Light, capital of the world.

Elsewhere in Europe, however, 1878 nearly saw the outbreak of a world war, caused, as the the war of 1914 was to be, by embroilments in the Balkans. The long disintegration of the Ottoman empire, which still sprawled over much of the area, had been accelerated since 1875 by revolts of many of her

Jean-Loup Charmet

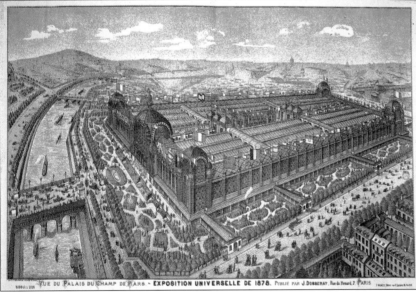

Jean-Loup Charmet

-VUE DU PALAIS DU CHAMP DE MARS.- EXPOSITION UNIVERSELLE DE 1878. PUBLIÉ PAR J.DOSSERAY, Rue du Renard, 7. PARIS

Tim Russell

The Trocadero Palace
(above) This housed the Exposition of 1878. Its exuberant architectural style symbolized the rebirth of Paris as a great city and centre of culture.

Cleopatra's needle
(right) This 3500-year-old Egyptian obelisk was moved to London in 1878. It is now a familiar landmark on the bank of the Thames.

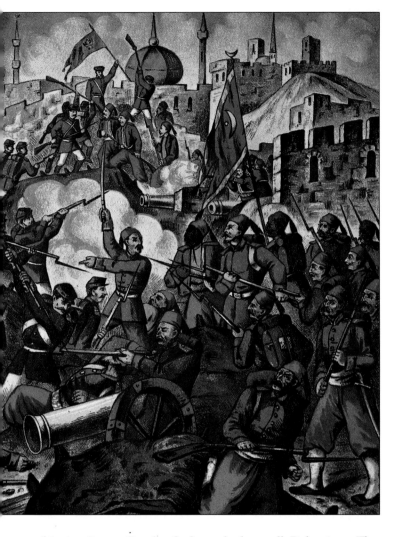

The fall of Adrianople
(left) This January victory for the advancing Russians opened the way for their seizure of a long-sought prize – Istanbul and the Straits. Only the presence of a British fleet made the Russians turn aside and instead set up a 'Big Bulgaria' satellite state. This, too, was unacceptable to the other Great Powers.

> *We don't want to fight but by Jingo if we do,*
> *We've got the men, we've got the ships, we've got*
> *the money too,*
> *We've fought the Bear before and while Britons*
> *shall be true,*
> *The Russians shall not have Constantinople.*

War was, however, averted by the Congress called in July at Berlin, capital of the new united Germany, by Bismark the German Chancellor. There Disraeli managed to play one power off against another in a dazzling display of diplomacy that gave almost all the countries concerned something of what they wanted – and kept the Russians away from the Aegean. He returned to London claiming he brought 'peace with honour'. In fact, this peace was to prove very fragile.

Another dispute ended less amicably that autumn in London. The American-born painter, James Whistler, had been enraged by the critic Ruskin's description of his painting, *Nocturne in Black and Gold*, as 'flinging a pot of paint in the public's face'. As Ruskin refused to retract, Whistler took him to

Irish agitation
(above) Charles Parnell addressing a meeting of the Irish Land League. Parnell, despite being a Protestant landowner, agitated to help the landless peasantry.

subject nations – Greeks, Serbs and, above all, Bulgarians. The Turks had reacted with a savage energy to crush the revolts. These 'Bulgarian massacres' were attacked with eloquently righteous indignation by the British statesman, William Gladstone in 1877. The Russians, then posing as defenders of their fellow Slavs, attacked the Turks with their massively superior armies.

WARM WATER PORTS

Despite a heroic defence by the Turks at Plevna, the Russians advanced steadily south, until they took Adrianople in January 1878. Ahead lay Constantinople (modern Istanbul), the Bosporus straits and access to what the landlocked Russians had long been scheming for – warm-water ports that could not easily be blockaded in time of war.

The British, who had gone to war in the Crimea 20 years earlier precisely to prevent such a happening, were thoroughly alarmed. The Prime Minister, Benjamin Disraeli, ordered the British fleet to Constantinople and called out the army reserve. The Austrians, who had their own ambitions in the Balkans, were also worried. Then in March came news of the Treaty of San Stefano which the Russians had forced the Turks to sign. This created a 'Big Bulgaria', stretching from the Black Sea to the Aegean and incorporating much of northern Greece, which would be garrisoned and governed by Russians. In Britain, the rising tide of anti-Russian feeling was reflected in the famous music-hall song:

Motley Books

Jean-Loup Charmet

court and won, receiving damages – of one farthing! Disgusted by England, and deeply in debt, Whistler left for Venice and Paris, where he would be better appreciated, though not by Mary Cassatt, who knew and thought little of his work. Cassatt had exhibited at the Third Impressionist Exhibition in 1877, and would do so again at the Fourth in 1879, but at the time 1878 was more notable in painting for the great *Life of St Genevieve* unveiled by the Symbolist master, Puvis de Chavannes.

In the US that year the first mass-produced bicycles were manufactured by A. A. Pope, while in London the earliest electric street lighting appeared to rival the old-established gaslights. The sphygmograph, which records the movements of the pulse, was first demonstrated in 1878.

In October, the Irish Land League was founded to agitate for relief for the wretched Irish peasantry. Its first President was Charles Parnell – apparently an odd choice, as Parnell was himself a Protestant landowner. But until his entanglement and disgrace in a divorce case in 1890, Parnell was to harrass the British Government mercilessly.

TROUBLES IN AFRICA

Far away in southern Africa, the last months of 1878 heralded fresh troubles for the British. The Zulus, a warrior confederacy that had been growing increasingly resentful of British encroachments on their territory, rejected an ultimatum delivered to them on 11 December and prepared for war. In January of the following year, they massacred an ill-prepared British army at Isandhlwana.

Further north, the incipient 'scramble for Africa', which was to occupy the European powers for the rest of the century, warmed up when the Belgians organized the Comité d'Etudes du Haut Congo to plan their advance into the interior. In Egypt, the government of the Khedive (king), whose

incompetence was matched only by its corruption, introduced a form of constitutional government in a bid to ward off the country's occupation – with little success, for within four years it had become a British colony in all but name. This annoyed the French, who considered they had an equal right to determine happenings in Egypt, having originally financed the Suez Canal, but it scarcely worried the Khedive, who was able to carry on his life of luxury little troubled by governmental cares.

John Singer Sargent: self-portrait/Aberdeen Art Gallery

JOHN SINGER SARGENT

1856-1925

John Singer Sargent was the most celebrated portrait painter of the Edwardian age. Born in Florence, his childhood was spent travelling from one European city or resort to another. He studied art in Paris and developed a realistic, traditional style, but he was also touched by the spirit of Impressionism. His natural fluency and the brilliant accuracy of his portraits brought him outstanding success in America and England.

When he became disillusioned with the demands of portraiture, Sargent concentrated on his mural and ceiling decorations for public buildings in Boston. He also travelled extensively, painting a vast number of landscape and figure subjects in oil and watercolour. An essentially shy and private man, he was charming and accomplished and, although he never married, was devoted to his family and circle of friends.

75

The Cultivated Expatriate

Sargent's incessant travelling took him to all the cultural centres of Europe. He emerged as an artist of dazzling ability and as a man of sophistication and awesome intelligence.

An expatriate family
Following the death of her first child, Mary Singer Sargent (far left) convinced her husband that they should leave America and embark on a European tour, as a restorative for her ailing spirit and health. So began 50 years of continual travel, with Mary giving birth to John in Florence in 1856, and to Emily in Rome in 1857 (left).

John Singer Sargent was born in Florence in January 1856, the son of American parents. His father, Dr Fitzwilliam Sargent, had studied medicine at the University of Pennsylvania and established a practice in Philadelphia when, in 1850, he married Mary Newbold Singer, the daughter of a wealthy Philadelphia fur merchant.

Mrs Sargent's very restless and romantic temperament was ill suited to the constraints of American provincial life and when, in 1853, the Sargents' first child died and Mrs Sargent's own health declined, the couple embarked for Europe in search of restoration. What began as a temporary scheme was to become a way of life – Dr Sargent gave up his medical practice and, on the strength of his wife's modest private income, they lived abroad permanently and raised a family.

The Sargents' expatriate existence was spent travelling from one city or resort to another. For John and his two sisters, Emily and Violet, it was an unconventional childhood. Their lack of roots meant that they were thrown in on themselves, encouraging in them an emotional independence. Emily suffered from a spinal complaint, which incapacitated her and thus isolated her to a greater

degree but she and John were particularly devoted to each other.

This life of travel gave Sargent a wide-ranging education although he had very little formal tuition. He grew up with a fluent command of Italian, spoke French and some German, was well read in European literature, was an accomplished pianist and a passionately keen musician. Art, history and foreign languages were not text book fodder, but aspects of the living culture which was unfolding around him.

TRAVEL SKETCHES

Sargent's drawing began as a way of documenting the sightseeing which occupied so much of the family's time. His mother, herself an amateur watercolourist, encouraged him to sketch the scenes of their travels and his surviving early sketchbooks contain drawings of plants and birds, architectural sketches and copies of the old masters. A noticeable quality of his early letters and drawings is his desire to describe his observations accurately.

The question of his future was somewhat

vexed. Dr Sargent had hopes of a naval career for his son, but it became apparent that he was determined to be a painter. He had received some instruction in Italy, but a more thorough training was necessary. Paris, with its *atelier* system, in which a group of students worked with a single master concentrating on drawing and painting from a living model, seemed to offer the best possibilities for study. The choice of the *atelier* of Carolus-Duran, a highly popular and successful portrait painter, was significant; it reflected the concern of Sargent's parents that their son's profession might be profitable.

Sargent's apprenticeship at the *atelier* on the Boulevard Montparnasse saw him applying the lessons of Carolus-Duran, learning to paint directly and realistically. He worked hard, absorbing both formal, traditional teaching and the new ideas with which Paris hummed. He enjoyed the life of the young art student and had numerous friends but few close attachments; he was considered by everyone who knew him to be modest, charming, accomplished and a lively and generous companion, but there was a reticence which kept him inviolably private, and so it was to be throughout his life.

In 1876, Sargent crossed the Atlantic for the first

Sargent: Portrait of Carolus-Duran/Sterling and Francine Clark Art Institute

Carolus-Duran
(*above*) *In 1874, Sargent entered the atelier of Carolus-Duran – one of the most sophisticated studios in Paris. Carolus himself, a distinguished portrait painter with several Salon medals, chose his students on the basis of 'unusual promise'. He taught his pupils to paint fluidly onto the canvas, without reworking, a method which encouraged the young Sargent's amazing technical facility.*

Niagara Falls
(*left*) *At the age of 20, John set foot on American soil for the first time, in the company of his mother and his favourite sister, Emily. Together they took in some of the major American sights, including Niagara Falls, which John recorded in a painting.*

Lauros-Giraudon

portrait was certainly influential in securing Sargent more portrait commissions because, hanging in White's Grosvenor Crescent House, it was seen by the London *beau monde*, among whom were many potential clients.

Painting Madame Gautreau, a fashionable Parisian beauty, notorious for her stunning, if unusual looks was, in contrast, a disaster. It was not a commissioned work; Sargent approached her through a friend to see if she would agree to let him paint her. He was fascinated by her dark, exotic beauty, the purity of her lines and her arresting profile. She was a difficult sitter but Sargent persevered, convinced that the picture would establish his reputation beyond doubt. Exhibited at the Salon in 1884 as *Madame X* (p.92), it caused a scandal; the critics and the public alike were alienated. This event unsettled Sargent and cast a shadow over his career in Paris.

Henry James, the American writer who lived in and was absorbed by Europe, met Sargent in Paris in 1884. He admired the artist's work and also admired Sargent himself, seeing him as something of a character from one of his own novels and

A home from home
In 1882, Sargent made a second visit to Venice and stayed with the Curtis family in the Palazzo Barbaro on the Grand Canal. The palazzo was a magnet for fellow expatriates, like Whistler and the novelist, Henry James.

time and visited America with his mother and Emily. Although cosmopolitan by upbringing and immersed in European culture, Sargent clung steadfastly to his American citizenship, so much so that he refused to relinquish it when he was offered a knighthood in 1907.

In the summer holidays, when classes at the *atelier* finished for the year, Sargent joined an informal group of fellow students to sketch and paint in the country. At Cancale in Brittany in 1877, he did *plein-air* sketches for his first important subject picture, *The Oyster Gatherers at Cancale* (p.82). It was to be his first success, winning him an honourable mention at the Paris Salon of 1878, and reflected his interest in the Impressionists.

STAR OF THE ATELIER

It was by now clear that Sargent was the star pupil at the *atelier*. Carolus-Duran was sufficiently impressed to allow Sargent to help him with work on a large ceiling decoration in the Louvre. Within the decorative scheme, Sargent painted a head of Carolus-Duran, which led to a formal three-quarter length portrait of his teacher. This won an honourable mention at the Salon of 1879 and it also signalled a turning point in Sargent's career; he was now a professional artist with his own studio, beginning to undertake commissions.

In 1883, Sargent moved to a more fashionable studio on the Boulevard Berthier and he painted Mrs Henry White, the wife of the First Secretary to the American Embassy in London. This arresting

The Inspiration of Spain and North Africa

In the Autumn of 1879, Sargent travelled to Spain. While in Madrid, he copied the paintings of Velázquez in the Prado, and their influence – expressed in a tauter and more austere style, a subdued tonality and a sense of the evocative possibilities of shadowy space – pervades much of his subsequent work; his Venetian interiors of 1880-82 and, most powerfully, *The Daughters of Edward D. Boit* (p.90). Sargent's imagination was always fired by the exotic and the bizarre; in Spain, Tangier and Morocco he responded to the colour and the drama of the people and landscape, painting the architecture and exploring the contrasts of brilliant light and cool shadows. His passionate interest in Spanish music and dance is realized in *El Jaleo* (pp.88-9).

AISA

describing him as being 'civilized to his fingertips'. When Sargent's future as a portrait painter in Paris seemed precarious, it was James who sang the attractions of London.

Sargent had been in England in 1884 and had painted a number of pictures of the Vickers family including several exquisitely lit, freely painted interiors. In 1885, he was again in England and with his fellow artist, Edwin Austin Abbey, took a boating trip on the Thames from Oxford to Windsor. They went on to Broadway in the Cotswolds and stayed at Farnham House, the home of the illustrator Frank Millet, where the atmosphere was sympathetic and the company stimulating and harmonious. Broadway was a lyrical passage for Sargent; he painted *plein-air* studies, more or less at random, setting up his easel and painting swiftly, fluidly, concentrating on the effects of colour and changing light.

In 1885, the break with Paris was complete, when Sargent moved into Whistler's old studio, 33 Tite Street in London. He sailed to America the following year, invited by the art collector, Henry Marquand, to paint his wife. America welcomed

Ormond Family Collection/photo: National Portrait Gallery, London

Moving up in the world
(above) As portrait commissions began to flow in more regularly, Sargent moved from the rough Latin quarter of Paris to a fashionable studio on the Boulevard Berthier, 'where', he wrote, 'I am better off'.

him with open arms, a one-man exhibition at the St Botolph Club in Boston was greeted with rapture, prestigious portrait commissions flooded in and discussions began about the project of mural decorations for the Boston Public Library. The artist began a lifelong friendship with Isabella Stewart Gardner, the flamboyant Boston hostess, who admired and collected his work.

THE SOCIETY PORTRAITIST

In America and in London, the 1890s were to see Sargent at the peak of his fame and reputation. *Lady Agnew* (p.94), exhibited at the Royal Academy in 1893, was hailed as a masterpiece and it established his position with the English art establishment. He became the artist sought by the *nouveaux riches*, who felt that their positions in society would be sanctioned by his brilliantly vivid translation of their characters in paint.

Towards the end of the 1890s, when Sargent was recognized as the supreme portrait painter of his age, the aristocracy, accustomed to being painted by the best, began to queue for his attentions and, in 1902, Rodin called him 'the Van Dyck of our times'. He moved towards a more formal style of painting, to the 'grand manner' of Reynolds, using props to suggest classical settings and aiming to create a timeless quality. He was overwhelmed with commissions, but his real enthusiasm lay elsewhere.

The Boston murals, first at the Public Library and later at the Museum of Fine Arts, preoccupied

Gift of Mrs Francis Ormond, 1950

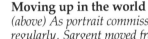
Sargent: Moorish Buildings in the Sunlight/Metropolitan Museum of Art, New York

Haunting rhythms
(left) A gifted musician himself, Sargent was captivated by the folk music and flamenco dancing of Spain, analysing gitano music in the same spirit as a student of musical theory. In Seville, he took notes and made sketches of singers and dancers in the tavernas.

Unfamiliar architecture
(above) After Spain, Sargent travelled to Tangier, where he wrote, 'We have rented a little Moorish house (which we don't yet know from any other house in the town, the little white tortuous streets are so exactly alike)'. Here, he made a number of oil sketches.

him from about 1890 until 1921, and involved him in intensive work in England and *in situ* in Boston and in a number of research expeditions to Egypt, Greece, Italy and the Holy Land. However, in spite of his dedication and effort, the murals lack passion and imaginative conviction. Sargent was excited by the visual world and the grand subjects of the murals demanded an emotional and imaginative key quite different from his own.

Sargent was now financially secure, but bored with portraiture. To Lady Radnor, he wrote in an uncompromising tone, 'Ask me to paint your gates, your fences, your barns, which I should gladly do, *but not the human face!*' By 1907 he was refusing all but a few commissions. His only concession was the charcoal sketch, which he could draw rapidly in a brief sitting and of which he executed a vast number. Released from the treadmill of portraiture, he was able to consult his own wishes and choose his own subjects.

HOLIDAYS IN THE ALPS

A new pattern emerged in Sargent's life. Each summer he would spend some three or four months travelling and sketching with Emily, Violet and her children and old artist friends. These sketching holidays would take them to the Alps, Purtud in the Val d'Aosta, or the Simplon Pass, moving down to Italy or Spain in the autumn. He returned repeatedly to Venice and painted numerous exquisite watercolours.

The shape of family life had gradually altered;

The Holy Land
(left) In 1890, Sargent was commissioned to decorate the Boston Public Library with murals illustrating the development of western religion. His exhaustive research expeditions took him as far as the Middle East, where he made this wonderful watercolour, Bedouins.

The Artist at War

When the First World War broke out, Sargent was staying in the Austrian Tyrol. At first, he seemed to be undisturbed by the increasing hostilities, but when his niece and her husband were killed in France, he began to feel emotionally involved. In 1918, he was asked by Lloyd George to journey to the Front as an official war artist, to paint an epic canvas commemorating the British and American effort. Sargent began by making sketches and watercolours of the soldiers marching, stealing fruit and undergoing treatment. But it was the sight of a group of men in a field, blinded by mustard gas, that inspired one of Sargent's finest works (pp.98-9).

The Interior of a Hospital Tent
(right) Sargent was more interested in the realities of war than in propaganda.

The Boston murals
(below) Sargent's murals for the Boston Library were intended to reflect the ideals of the American Renaissance, in their elevated depiction of the classical past. Pagan Deities: Astarte and Neith, *on the north ceiling, was one of the more successful images, giving Americans a flavour of the new Symbolist aesthetic.*

his father died in 1889 and Violet had married in 1891, but it was the death of his mother in 1905 which had the most profound effect. Emily was now effectively alone and, always exceptionally close, she and her brother became the centre of each other's worlds. She was Sargent's hostess, his confidante, the only person who knew him fully and the only woman to whom he committed himself even though his remarkably tranquil emotional life had been punctuated with speculation about marriage. In the early 1880s, there had been strong rumour of an engagement to Louise Burckhardt, the *Lady with the Rose* (p.83), and, in later life, gossip surrounded his friendships with Mrs Gardner and Mrs Charles

Sketching holidays
(above) In the latter part of his life, Sargent spent most of his summers in the Alps, at Purtud in the Val d'Aosta, or the Simplon Pass, sketching and making watercolours of the magnificent scenery or relaxing with members of his family and close friends.

Hunter, the generous and indefatigable hostess and art collector, who was, apart from Emily, the person to whom he was closest.

The First World War took Sargent to France as an official war artist. He showed a remarkable lack of fear when under direct fire, but he remained at one remove from the horror emotionally, his obsession with observing what he saw with the eyes of a painter in its way protecting him from the full impact. The war had, however, touched him personally when the husband of his niece, Rose-Marie, and then Rose-Marie herself were killed.

He continued to work on the Boston decorations, noting to a friend, 'Now the American things are done, and so I suppose, I may die when I like'. In April 1925, he booked passage to America to accompany the last panels. Emily held a farewell dinner for him, inviting Violet and several of his closest friends; it was a happy, relaxed occasion. The following morning Sargent was found in bed, a volume of Voltaire's *Dictionnaire Philosophique* open before him. He had died of a heart attack and he was buried at Brookwood Cemetery, Surrey.

The Modern Portraitist

**Sargent's work shows the influence of Impressionism combined
with his fluent style and rich sense of colour. Despite his reputation
as a portraitist, Sargent painted many other subjects.**

Museum of Fine Arts, Boston

**The Oyster Gatherers
at Cancale**
*(left) Sargent first used
Carolus-Duran's method
out-of-doors in Cancale,
Brittany, in 1877. This
painting was the result,
winning a second class
medal at the Paris Salon
a year later.*

Lady with a Rose
*(right) This was the
portrait of Charlotte
Louise Burckhardt aged
19. Her mother was keen
on making a match
between her and Sargent,
but although he seemed
fond of her, nothing came
of it. The portrait borrows
its composition from
Velázquez and was praised
as 'everything one could
possibly wish.'*

The wide range of Sargent's work is not generally
realized, as he is primarily known as a portraitist.
In fact, he painted landscapes, formal subject
pictures, figure studies, even murals, using
watercolours as well as oils.

It was in Paris, under the supervision of
Carolus-Duran, that Sargent began to develop his
remarkable fluency. Carolus-Duran insisted that
his students paint *au premier coup* (at the first touch,
no reworking), encouraging rapid and fluid
execution. He was concerned with creating
realistic effects by painting objects accurately in
terms of their tonal values, applying the middle
tones first and then building up the lights and
darks around them.

Carolus-Duran was a devotee of Velázquez,
then all the rage in the Paris *ateliers*, and he used to
intone his name as he wandered around the
studio. Sargent's early Paris portraits show him as
the supreme exponent of his teacher's methods as,
in a style elegant, spare and restrained, he was able
both to suggest nuance of character and create
brooding atmosphere.

Frans Hals was the artist who, other than
Velázquez, had a profound effect on Sargent's
technique. Sargent visited Haarlem in 1880 and
was stunned by Hals's expressiveness, his verve

and bravura, and the economy of his brushwork. It
is often in Sargent's more informal sketches, which
seem to catch a fleeting expression, that Hals's
virtuoso handling is most apparent.

In the 1870s, Carolus-Duran was regarded as a
modernist; he was a friend of Manet, and he was in
touch with the new ideas which were sweeping
Paris. Several of Sargent's early landscape studies
reflect the Impressionists' concern with the effect
of light but, at this early stage in his career, he was
chiefly occupied with portrait work and had little
opportunity to work *en plein air*. The late 1870s
show a revival of his interest; he painted a series of
landscapes in Brittany and Nice, in which he used
a lighter palette and freer, more broken
brushwork. He exhibited with the Societé des
Viṅgts (Les XX), a progressive group, in Brussels
in 1884 and he was, with Monet, involved in the
effort to buy Manet's *Olympia* for the Louvre.

It was England, however, which saw the
flowering of Sargent's Impressionist phase. In the
congenial, pastoral setting of Broadway in the
summer of 1885, he devoted himself to *plein-air*
experiments. Edmund Gosse remembered
Sargent taking out his easel, putting it down
wherever the mood took him and simply painting
what he saw, 'the painter's business being, not to

Metropolitan Museum of Art. Bequest of Mrs Valerie B Hadden

Ormond Family Collection/photo: National Portrait Gallery, London

The Brook

(above) The girls resting by the brook are Sargent's nieces, Violet's daughters Reine (left) and Rose-Marie (both in Turkish dress), who often posed for him on their holidays together in Italy and Switzerland. Rose-Marie was his favourite model – she was tragically killed at the age of 24 in the German bombardment of France.

Breakfast in the Loggia

(below) In the autumn of 1910, Sargent was lent the Villa Torre Galli near Florence, where he was joined by several friends. The loggia features in several studies. Here it provides the setting for Sargent's observation of light effects in which the figures of Jane de Glehn and Eliza Wedgwood, in leisurely conversation, play a secondary role.

Freer Gallery of Art/Smithsonian Institution

pick and choose, but to render the effect before him, whatever it may be. His daily plan was to cover the whole of his canvas with a thin coat of colour, so as to make a complete sketch which would dry so rapidly that next morning he might paint another study over it. I often could have wept to see the brilliantly fresh and sparkling sketches ruthlessly sacrificed.' The surviving studies vibrate with light and sensuous colour, the brushwork is bold and jagged in an uninhibited, Impressionistic manner.

FRIENDSHIP WITH MONET

Sargent spent the summer of 1888 at Calcot, on the Thames, and that of 1889 at Fladbury, on the Avon. The riverside pictures of this period have a specific Impressionist resonance; they recall Claude Monet. Sargent had probably met Monet as early as 1876 but, thereafter, details about their friendship are hazy, until the late 1880s, when they seem to have become closer; Sargent visited Giverny, Monet's house in Normandy, bought four of his paintings and painted three portraits of Monet. The riverside scenery had natural Monetesque associations and Sargent's treatment of light on water in these studies is particularly

83

Aristocratic portraits

The genre of aristocratic portraits in England was established by Van Dyck. He created an informal but elegant style which flattered his sitters and accentuated their social status by emphasising their rich clothing and palatial surroundings. The English portraitist Lawrence and the American, Copley, were both heirs to this tradition. Unlike them, however, Sargent painted numerous middle-class sitters; in portraying them, his style is simpler and more direct, and concentrates less on the sitters' surroundings.

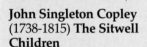

Renishaw Hall, Derbyshire

John Singleton Copley (1738-1815) **The Sitwell Children**
(above) In Copley's portrait, the Sitwells' neo-classical drawing-room is painted with as much attention to detail as the sitters. The lively informality of the children owes much to Reynolds.

Sir Thomas Lawrence (1769-1830) **The Countess of Blessington**
The easy grace and bravura brushwork of the portrait of the Countess in décolleté show Van Dyck's influence. Lawrence earned his fame with a portrait of the Queen.

Wallace Collection, London

brilliant. His pictures of his sister, Violet, against the river background echo Monet's series of girls with parasols standing against the sky, but there is a clear distinction – Sargent was never to take the preoccupations of Impressionism to their logical conclusions. His figures are represented more traditionally and they retain an identity and an integrity within his Impressionistic compositions.

NEW SUBJECTS

The effect of these experiments on Sargent's portraits emerged in looser, richer brushwork, a lighter range of colour and a vitality and lightness of touch. After the turn of the century, when portraiture had begun to pall, Sargent began to devote more of his time to subject matter which pleased his eye and engaged his interest. He painted oils and watercolours of architectural details, palm trees, a classical statue or a group of Bedouin, all reflecting his intense curiosity about the visual world. Believing that mural decoration was the highest form of art, his work on the Boston murals absorbed much of his creative energy from

Tate Gallery, London

TRADEMARKS

Fluid brushwork

Sargent's extraordinary facility with the brush resulted in a variety of textures and a marvellous fluidity of line in his paintings. His brushwork did not vary much when using watercolours and oils.

Claude Monet Painting at the Edge of a Wood *(left and detail below) This painting shows Sargent's debt to Monet in his loose style of brushwork, seen here on Monet's palette (detail), and his impression of a scene* en plein air. *But Sargent could not go to the extremes that the Impressionists went. When painting with Monet in Giverny, Sargent asked to borrow some black. When Monet replied he did not have any, Sargent cried 'Then I can't paint' – he needed black to model form. Sargent had boundless admiration for Monet however, and bought four of his paintings.*

1890 onwards. Grand and complex, they emerge as curiously lifeless, and posterity has largely forgotten them.

Sargent's sitters remembered him as an energetic, expressive painter; he would walk slowly back from the easel for some distance, gazing at the sitter and the canvas as he did so, and then he would run and lunge at the canvas again, placing the next, precise brushstroke, often muttering his favourite 'Pish-tosh!' or 'Demons!' as he did so. He drew with a large brush, well loaded with paint, building up the figure from the background in sweeping movements; William Rothenstein, a fellow artist, described him painting in 'large, loose volumes of shadow, half-tones and light, regardless of features or refinements of form, finally bringing the masses of light and shade together and thus assembling the figure', summary of Carolus-Duran's teaching.

This is the advice Sargent passed on to students at the Royal Academy Schools; he also stressed the importance of cultivating 'an ever continuous power of observation' and, in a sentence which suggests something of his own driving force, he urged them: 'Above all things get abroad, see the sunlight, and everything that is to be seen . . .'

THE MAKING OF A MASTERPIECE

Carnation, Lily, Lily, Rose

This picture was painted in the autumns of 1885 and 1886, at Farnham House and Russell House, the successive Broadway homes of Frank Millet and his family. The two girls, Dorothy and Polly, daughters of the artist Frederick Barnard and his wife Alice, posed in specially made white dresses and, when the flowers in the garden faded, Sargent transplanted rose beds and sent new lilies to be planted in pots to retain the luxuriant background. It was executed entirely in the open air and, as the twilight was of such short duration, the easel, canvas and models had to be standing in readiness each evening for that particular light to appear.

Tate Gallery, London

A problematic subject
(left) Sargent expressed his difficulties with his subject matter to Emily thus: 'Impossible brilliant colours of flowers and lamps and brightest green lawn background. Paints are not bright enough.'

Polly and Dorothy Barnard
(below) These are pencil sketches of Sargent's two models aged 7 and 11. They replaced the younger Kate Millet who first posed for the picture. Being dark, Kate had to

wear a blonde wig, but the Barnard sisters had the advantage of fair hair. They were also older and therefore less likely to move around while the artist was at work, (which, in any case, was only the duration of dusk).

Tate Gallery, London

Tate Gallery, London

By lantern light
(*right*) *Sargent first saw paper lanterns hung among trees and flowers when he was resting in Pangbourne after a diving accident, and the effect of the light charmed him. Then in Broadway, he began the painting of 'two little girls in a garden at dusk, lighting paper lanterns hung among the flowers'. Capturing the different types of light was all important to him. The artificial light of the lanterns glows in the dusk, reflecting on the faces, dresses and hands of the little girls.*

Garden Study of the Vickers Children
(*below*) *Sargent stayed with Albert Vickers (of the great engineering family) at Lavington Rectory, Sussex, in 1884. His painting of the two children watering the tall lilies anticipates the mood and idea of* Carnation, Lily, Lily, Rose.

Flint Institute of Arts, Michigan

When I was painting my own 'mug', I decided to devote myself to other branches of art . . .

Sargent

Sargent at work
(*right*) *This caricature by Millet shows Sargent working on 'Darnation, Silly, Silly, Pose,' as Sargent later renamed the painting. It aptly bears out Edmund Gosse's description: 'Instantly he took his place at a distance from the canvas and at a certain notation of the light, ran forward over the lawn with the action of a wagtail, planting at the same time rapid dabs of paint on the picture and then retiring again, only with equal suddenness to repeat the wagtail action.'*

Gallery

Sargent was the greatest and most successful society portraitist of his era, painting the rich and famous with an elegance and flair that no contemporary artist could match. He responded intuitively to the individuality of each sitter, but was undoubtedly at his best with beautiful women, and the incisive Madame X and the meltingly sensuous Lady

El Jaleo *1882*
94½″ × 137″ Isabella Stewart Gardner Museum, Boston

'Jaleo' is a word meaning 'uproar', indicating a party. Sargent had visited Spain in 1879-80 and made sketches there on which the picture is based, but a Frenchwoman, Marie Renard, later modelled for the dancer. There was a vogue for Spanish art and Spanish subjects in France, and Sargent had an enormous success with this picture at the 1882 Salon, one contemporary review describing him as 'the most talked-about painter in Paris'. The painting's powerful contrasting tones acknowledge Manet, but here Sargent is translating Manet's almost brutal extremism into theatre.

Agnew show how varied his approach could be. Sargent also had a great gift for depicting children, as The Daughters of Edward D. Boit and Carnation, Lily, Lily, Rose memorably demonstrate. Sargent's accomplishments extended beyond portraiture. He was a consummate master of the watercolour technique, with a particular flair for landscape, and El Jaleo, the most famous of his early works, is a splendidly vivacious dance scene. But it is his war paintings that reveal the most unexpected side to his talents. Gassed – grave, monumental and compassionate – is undoubtedly one of the finest war paintings of the 20th century.

The Daughters of Edward D. Boit *1882*
87″ × 87″ Museum of Fine Arts, Boston

Sargent painted the portrait in the Paris home of the American artist, Edward Darley Boit. It is an unusual setting, with the two enormous Chinese vases emerging from the gloom. For the composition, Sargent was indebted to some extent to Velázquez's celebrated royal group portrait Las Meninas, *which he had copied in Spain. The composition has strong geometrical accents and is lit by light streaming in from the left. There is a deliberate lack of relationship between the figures. The girls' white dresses, standing out against the predominantly dark surroundings, show once again Sargent's preoccupation with tonal contrast.*

Carnation, Lily, Lily, Rose *1885-6*
68½″ × 60½″ Tate Gallery, London

The title comes from a popular song of the time entitled The Wreath.
*The subject compares with the scenes of childhood, like those of
Millais, which had such great appeal for the Victorians. But Sargent
treats the figures and flowers in an Impressionist manner tempered by
poetic and decorative considerations. He was particularly concerned
to capture the fleeting light of dusk and its effects, and since he only
worked on it at twilight, the painting took a long time to complete.
For all the labour that went into it, it has a marvellous quality of
freshness which has contributed to its success.*

Madame X (Madame Pierre Gautreau) *1884*
82½" × 43¼" Metropolitan Museum of Art, New York

This is probably Sargent's best-known portrait, mainly on account of the scandal it caused when it was exhibited at the Paris Salon in 1884. Madame Gautreau was an American who had married a wealthy Parisian banker. When Sargent met her he was so struck by her outlandishly unconventional beauty that he spared no efforts to persuade her to sit for him. The portrait was attacked by some on aesthetic grounds, as its exaggerated and stylized pose was thought ugly, but the main criticism was directed at the brazen and provocative attitude of Madame Gautreau and her low-cut dress, held to indicate moral laxity. (Although she was not named as the sitter, her identity was no secret.) Her mother was so appalled at the event that she asked Sargent to remove the portrait from exhibition ('My daughter is lost – all Paris laughs at her', she told him), but he refused. In the wake of the scandal, Sargent moved to London.

Ellen Terry as Lady Macbeth *1889*
87" × 45" Tate Gallery, London (on loan to National Portrait Gallery)

Ellen Terry was one of the most celebrated actresses in the history of the British theatre. Sargent saw her as Lady Macbeth at the Lyceum Theatre in London in December 1888 and was greatly impressed with her performance. When he had arranged for her to sit for her portrait, he spent some time deciding how he would represent her before settling on this grandly rhetorical pose. As memorable as the forceful characterization is the virtuoso painting of the costume, which shows Sargent's brushwork at its lushest. Many of Sargent's finest portraits are, as this one is, more or less life-size full-lengths; like his great predecessors in society portraiture such as Van Dyck and Gainsborough, he had the self-confidence and the panache to paint such grandiose images with magnificent assurance, even though the apparently unhesitating flourish of his brushwork often concealed much labour and some reworking.

Lady Agnew *c.1892-3*
49½″ × 39½″ National Gallery of Scotland, Edinburgh

This ravishing painting won great acclaim at the 1893 Royal Academy exhibition in London. The enthusiasm is easy to understand, for Lady Agnew's beauty and grace are wonderfully captured and the exquisite colour harmonies of mauve and white in her costume are among the loveliest Sargent ever created.

The Wyndham Sisters *1899*
114″ × 84″ Metropolitan Museum of Art, New York

*The sitters were the daughters of the Hon. Percy Wyndham and the
portrait was painted in his London home in Belgrave Square. They were
renowned for their talent and beauty and when the picture was
exhibited at the Royal Academy, Edward VII dubbed it 'The Three
Graces'. The composition shows Sargent's skill in arranging figures.*

Pomegranates 1908
21" × 14½" The Brooklyn Museum, New York

In his watercolours, Sargent favoured subjects that were completely different from formal portraits. This subject was painted on Majorca and featured later in the 'Messianistic Eva' lunette for the Boston Library, the pomegranate being a symbol of the unified Church in Christian mythology and rejuvenation in pagan lore.

Mountain Stream c.1910-12
13½" × 21" Metropolitan Museum of Art, New York

Sargent travelled much, particularly in Italy, in the period in which this watercolour was painted, but the location of the scene is unknown. In technique it has a sparkling freshness that is completely appropriate to the subject, the figure simply acting as another contrasting texture in the landscape.

Gassed *1918-19*
90½″ × 240″ Imperial War Museum, London

*In July 1918, Sargent went to France to paint a war picture for the
Ministry of Information. He had difficulty in finding a suitable
subject but, one evening, he went with the artist Henry Tonks to see a
dressing station and found a group of men, blinded by mustard gas,
waiting to be treated, who became his inspiration. Much of Sargent's
experience with the Boston murals informed this painting, especially
the Prophets' frieze where the figures are linked together by gestures.
The desolation of the trench zone is evoked, while the stumbling men
touch on nightmare.*

The Broadway Group

The village of Broadway, Worcestershire is today – as it was a century ago – a popular place for visitors. It was the chosen idyllic spot of an American artistic colony who made it their home in the 1880s.

Sargent paid his first visit to Broadway in September 1885 to recuperate from a bad head wound received while diving from a weir. He had been invited to go to this little Worcestershire village by his friend, the American painter Edwin Austin Abbey. Broadway, then little known and remote from the railway, was the home of a small colony of artists, many of whom were, like Sargent, expatriate Americans. It was here that Sargent painted what was later to become one of his best loved pictures, *Carnation, Lily, Lily, Rose*.

Broadway was 'discovered' by the American illustrator and painter Francis Millet, in 1885. It was then – and still is – an idyllic spot at the extreme south-eastern corner of Worcestershire, tucked into the foot of the Cotswolds overlooking the Vale of Evesham. Its long main street, lined with 16th and 17th-century stone cottages, leads to the village green. This was the view that prompted the biographer and novelist E. V. Lucas, to write of the 'wide, long, grass-bordered vistas of brownish-grey cottages, thatched, latticed, mottled, mended, ivied, immemorial. It is hardly surprising that this quintessentially English rural charm should have cast its spell on the American visitors.'

C. C. Houghton Collection, Broadway

Du Maurier: F. D. Millet

Between Two Fires
(above) Before crossing the Atlantic, Millet had led an extremely varied and active public life both in America and in Europe, including working as an author, illustrator and war correspondent. He was a competent painter, but not outstanding, and this humorous scene is a typical example.

RURAL HAVEN

The last few decades of the 19th century had witnessed a vogue for artists' colonies. In Britain alone, groups of artists gravitated to remote parts of the country where they could work in picturesque rural or romantic surroundings, well away from the dirt and the noise of the cities. Around the time that Broadway was in its heyday, other artists had occupied Newlyn in Cornwall, Whitby in Yorkshire and Walberswick in Suffolk. Echoing the French Impressionists, much of whose work was painted in the countryside, artists in England aimed to capture the fleeting effect of light and shade in pastoral surroundings.

Francis Millet and his family first moved to Farnham House, which overlooked the village green in Broadway. They acquired this along with a 14th-century monastic ruin known as Abbot's Grange which they restored and converted into a

Founding of Broadway
(above and right) Francis Millet was the first to discover the rural charm of Broadway and chose to settle there from America in 1885, with his family. Their first home was Farnham House at the bottom of the village green (right), a typical old Broadway house built of Cotswold stone. It was not long before a large and distinguished crowd of artistic and literary friends followed Millet's example in the choice of Broadway as a perfect country retreat.

C. C. Houghton Collection, Broadway

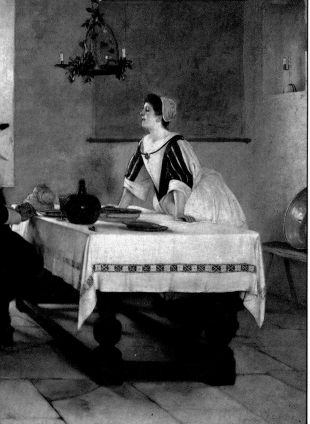

Tate Gallery, London

studio. Millet was soon joined by a host of English and American friends, namely the painters Edwin Abbey, Sargent, George Boughton, Alfred Parsons (illustrator of Dickens' work), Edwin Blashfield, the English illustrator Fred Barnard and the writers Henry James and Edmund Gosse.

With the sole exception of Henry James, the friends had a talent for the unruly, semi-bohemian hospitality that was fashionable among artists at the time. They were a strangely assorted company, colourful and noisy, but above all united in intellectual and artistic interests. They frequently shattered the calm of the village with their high

spirits, as is described here by Edmund Gosse: 'Nothing we do scandalizes the villagers. Fred Barnard, with an enormous stage slouch hat over his shoulders, chased one of the Americans down the village street, the man chased screaming all the time and trying to escape up lamp-posts and down wells. Not a villager smiled . . . Whatever we do or say or wear or sing they only say "Them Americans is out again".'

HIGH SPIRITS

Letters written by the Broadway residents and visitors are our main source of information about the high-spirited lifestyle there. A certain amount of serious work was done, but this was well interspersed with tennis, tea, musical evenings, dances and tennis again. In 1886, Gosse wrote a description of Abbot's Grange, and the new use to which it was being put: 'A mediaeval ruin, a small ecclesiastical edifice, which was very roughly repaired so as to make a kind of refuge for us, and there, in the morning, Henry James and I would write, while Abbey and Millet painted on the floor below, and Sargent and Parsons tilted their easels just outside. We were all within shouting distance, and not much serious work was done, for we were in towering spirits and everything was food for laughter. Henry James was the only sedate one of all – benign, indulgent but grave, and not often unbending beyond a genial chuckle.'

Another letter, written by Edwin Abbey, tells more: 'Millet is painting two interiors, Barnard is doing various sketches, and I've been painting a little watercolour of a very draughty church. There are three models down from town all eating their

Abbot's Grange
(below) The Broadway group made their studio in one of the oldest domestic buildings in Worcestershire – a 14th-century priory known as Abbot's Grange, just around the corner from Farnham House. Although somewhat derelict, the building was quite large and made an ideal studio.

C. C. Houghton Collection, Broadway

heads off today . . . F. Anstey Guthrie is coming this week to stay with us awhile, and later on Austin Dobson.'

When visitors came to stay, they frequently lodged at the Lygon Arms, a dominating and beautiful 16th-century former manor house at the edge of the Green. Sargent stayed there at first, as did Abbey, who used some of the details of the building in the backgrounds to his illustrations to Goldsmith's play *She Stoops to Conquer*.

Music was a great source of pleasure to the friends. Abbey wrote, 'We have music until the house won't stand it. Sargent is going elaborately through Wagner's trilogy, recitatives and all . . . Miss Gertrude Giswold sings to us like an angel.' There are also tales of games and dancing: 'We really do have a gay summer, pretending to work and sometimes working . . . until four, and then tennis until dinner time, and after dinner, dancing and music and various cheering games in the studio, but mostly dancing.' In such a frivolous atmosphere it is hardly surprising that the

Tate Gallery, London

A successful career
(above and right) Edwin Austin Abbey began as an illustrator in Philadelphia, where he worked for Harper's magazine. He moved to England in his early 20s and illustrated a number of plays, including She Stoops to Conquer *by Oliver Goldsmith, shown above. His paintings (one shown right) owe a debt to Pre-Raphaelite artists, but have their own particularly decorative treatment. Abbey had a successful artistic career both in England, where his works were shown at the Royal Academy, and in America where, with Sargent, he was commissioned to paint murals for the Boston Public Library.*

Abbey: O Mistress Mine. Walker Art Gallery, Liverpool

community were fundamentally artificial, and eventually this became apparent. Abbey had met his wife, Mary, in 1888, when they were both guests of the Millets at Russell House in Broadway. They went to America together, returning as a married couple in 1890, but not to so sunny an atmosphere as before. Mary, who was an outspoken, dominating woman and rather frosty in her manner, felt the unbuttoned communal life at Broadway was not sufficiently serious for her husband. She even doubted that the others had the appropriate respect of Abbey's work. And she wanted to be mistress in her own home.

During his stay in America Abbey had, with Sargent, been commissioned to paint a large mural cycle for Boston Public Library. He had planned to execute these in Broadway, but his wife had other ideas. Instead of remaining with the community, and their narrow, illustrators' horizons, Mary and Edwin Abbey bought an old English country house in Fairford, 40 miles south of Broadway. There they were followed by Sargent, and, in time, by Henry James. The heart, and the major artistic driving force, were thus removed from Broadway, and as an artistic community it faded.

Perhaps Henry James, who had throughout remained characteristically a little detached from the others, should have the last word about Broadway before the idyll was finally shattered: ' Furnished apartments are useful to the artist, but a furnished country is even more so . . . This is the great recommendation of Broadway: everything in it is convertible . . . There is portraiture in the air and composition in the very accidents. Everything is a subject or an effect . . . It is delicious to be at Broadway and not have to draw.'

Broadway colony produced few outstanding works, and only Sargent's *Carnation, Lily, Lily, Rose* can be considered a masterpiece.

The lush Worcestershire countryside had other charms than to be subjects for pictures. Almost every afternoon Henry James and Edmund Gosse would go for walks in the Vale of Evesham where they would take the gentle, level walks to the west, rather than the steep Broadway Hill to the east of the village. A favourite destination was Aston Somerville, a hamlet some two miles from Broadway. As James and Gosse sauntered towards it – and James always sauntered, on account of a weakness in his back muscles – James would regularly remark that Aston was 'so Italian, so Tuscan', as though he were coming across it for the first time.

On other days, groups of the friends with their wives and children, would have rollicking expeditions rowing down the Avon from Evesham to Pershore. On one particular trip, Gosse tells of Edwin Abbey playing the banjo, with everyone – except Henry James – singing as they rowed along. James sat alone 'like a beneficent deity, a sort of bearded Buddha, at the prow, manifestly a little afraid that some of us would tumble into the river.'

The infectious high spirits of the Broadway

Rural tranquility
(above) The peace of the surrounding Cotswold countryside provided a contrast to the group's boisterous lifestyle. The wooded footpaths of the Vale of Evesham were especially popular for gentle afternoon strolls and idle conversation.

Henry James
(right) Henry James was a prominent member of the Broadway group, but was somewhat aloof. His self-assurance is described here by Sargent's biographer, Olson: 'Henry James was like a great queen-bee; wherever he went he was utterly confident the swarm would follow'.

Sargent: Henry James. National Portrait Gallery, London

A Year in the Life 1918

While Sargent was sketching on the Western Front, American intervention was about to decide the war in the Allies' favour. Although Germany was victorious in Eastern Europe, she failed to deliver a knock-out blow in the West and, with loss of morale and the capitulation of her allies, was forced to acknowledge defeat.

By 1918, the strain of war was beginning to tell on civilians and combatants alike. Britain had her first experience of rationing, but there was no widespread discontent except in Ireland, where an attempt to apply conscription laws failed dismally. In central Europe, where the British naval blockade was causing much suffering and some actual starvation, there were signs of distress and strikes became common. The long-term outlook for the Central Powers was gloomier, since the United States of America had entered the war in April 1917 and by the summer of 1918 would be pouring armies into the Western Front. Also, thanks to the United States, the Allies had even acquired a moral advantage: in January 1918, President Woodrow Wilson enunciated his Fourteen Points, calling for a settlement based on national self-determination.

America's decisive intervention
(left) It was America's support of the British and the French which tipped the balance decisively in their favour in 1918. When they entered the war, the Americans believed it was to preserve the principles of democracy threatened by German aggression. But recruitment was slow at first and the powerful, if crude, imagery of war propaganda was necessary even across the Atlantic.

The Red Baron
(right) The war saw the first use of aerial combat which was often undertaken with great chivalry. The German aristocrat, Baron Manfred von Richtofen was one such 'knight' of the air whose nickname derived from the colour of his aircraft. The magazine announcing his death in May proclaimed, 'He is dead, but his spirit lives on.'

Imperial War Museum

Germany's only hope was to end the war in the east and use all her forces to defeat Britain and France before the Americans arrived. In March, this still seemed possible. The Bolsheviks had come to power in Russia, promising 'Peace and Bread' to an exhausted people and shattered armies. At Brest-Litovsk they accepted harsh German terms, signing away vast territories in order to gain a breathing-space. However, Russia remained an outcast among the nations and before the end of the year, Japanese, British, French and other foreign armies had been landed to unseat the Bolsheviks and support their 'White' enemies. During the consequent upheavals, the imprisoned Tsar and his family were shot by the Bolsheviks.

On 21 March, the Germans began their bid to end the war quickly, but although Ludendorf's two offensives won some striking successes, they soon petered out. Moreover an epidemic of 'Flanders fever', the influenza that was sweeping round the world, broke out and was to take even more lives than the war itself. Then, in July and August, the Allies hit back using hundreds of tanks. For the first time the German forces failed to hold firm.

THE LAST DAYS OF THE WAR

Even so, the Germans retreated and dug in on the Siegfried Line. But by October the end was in sight as, one after another, Germany's allies collapsed. The British and Serbs knocked out Bulgaria, the Italians defeated the Austrians at Vittorio Veneto, and the Turks were driven from Palestine. Germany and

The war artists
(left) The futility and savagery of war was depicted by artists from both sides. However, the British artists – all serving men – may well rank as the best exponents. Paul Nash, who painted The Ypres Salient at Night *(1918) produced some extraordinarily powerful work at this time which brought home the desolation of trench warfare.*

Intercepting the Turkish retreat
(above) Germany's allies, the Turks were fiercely routed from Palestine in 1918 by the advancing British army of General Allenby, while the RAF caught the retreating enemy columns negotiating the tricky ravines. The Destruction of the Turkish Transport by Sidney Carline was painted as a reconstruction in 1919.

Austria-Hungary asked for an armistice but, before it was signed on 11 November, revolution swept across central Europe. The Grand Fleet mutinied at Kiel and the Kaiser abdicated. And, as whole provinces of Austria-Hungary were incorporated into the new states of Poland, Czechosloakia and Yugoslavia, the Habsburg Empire simply fell apart. A new German democratic republic hoped for generous terms under the Fourteen Points. But, in Britain, Lloyd George held a snap general election (the first in which women over 30 were given the vote) which was fought with ominous slogans such as 'Hang the Kaiser' and 'Make the Hun Pay'.

Most important events in 1918 were directly or indirectly connected with the World War. In its aftermath, King Nicholas of Montenegro was deposed and his dominions became part of newly-created Yugoslavia. In Portugal, the pro-German dictator, General Sidonio Paes, was assassinated. And the immense vogue enjoyed by Oswald Spengler's *Decline of the West* reflected the cultural pessimism of 1918: this was an obscurely written historical work, which analysed the rise and decay of cultures, and caught the popular imagination with its assertion that the West had now entered its final phase.

The arts and sciences, though often exploited for warlike purposes, continued to develop independently. In 1918, the Original Dixieland Jazz Band crossed the Atlantic and brought a new kind of music – jazz – to Europe; and Lytton Strachey, a Bloomsburyite and conscientious objector, published an unlikely best seller in *Eminent Victorians*, which started a fashion for the 'debunking' of revered historical figures.

A doomed family
(right) In the spring of 1918, the Imperial family of Nicholas II was moved to Ekaterinburg in the Urals. The Czar had abdicated the year before. Imprisoned in a house around which a fence had been hastily built, the Romanovs came to an abrupt and brutal end in the early hours of 17 July, shot at point blank range.

Fotomas Index

Jean-Loup Charmet

Dancing in the streets
(left) The war ended on 11 November 1918 – Armistice Day. After months of war-weariness, the news was received with spontaneous jubilation and a carnival atmosphere prevailed for several days. France was liberated and the victorious Allied troops were greeted on the streets of Paris with a grateful euphoria.

Josephine N. Hopper Bequest

Self-Portrait 1925-30/Whitney Museum of American Art New York

EDWARD HOPPER
1882-1967

Born in 1882 in Nyack, near New York City, Edward Hopper is the greatest painter of modern American life yet to emerge. He studied painting in New York with Robert Henri, founder of the Ashcan School. On leaving college, he became a commercial artist, only giving up this career at the age of 42 to become a full-time artist. His interest in the effects of light was inspired by the Impressionists, whose work he saw in Paris.

Hopper found his very distinctive style in the 1920s and hardly changed it at all from then on. Although he lived through the heyday of abstraction, Hopper remained committed to the tradition of representational painting. Despite his late start, America was quick to heap honours upon him. But he remained a very private man, leading a life dedicated to painting with his wife, a fellow artist. Hopper died in 1967, aged 84.

The Austere American

**Tall and laconic, Edward Hopper liked to think of himself as
a down-to-earth, self-made man. He cherished his personal privacy,
preferring silence to idle chatter and artistic pretension.**

Edward Hopper grew up in middle-class small-town America. He was born on 22 July 1882 in Nyack, on the Hudson River just above New York City, the son of a shopkeeper. He later described his father as 'an incipient intellectual who never quite made it'. Edward was a solitary, bookish boy, who stood apart from other children because of his abnormal height – he suddenly grew to six feet at the age of 12. The Hoppers' home overlooked the Hudson, and Eddie, as he was then called,

developed an early enthusiasm for boats, building his own cat-boat at 15 with wood and tools supplied by his father.

Encouraged by his mother, Hopper soon began to demonstrate a precocious talent for drawing and, at the age of 17, he entered the Correspondence School of Illustrating in New York. The following year he transferred to the New York School of Art, studying first illustration and then painting. He found himself among an exceptionally gifted generation of students, including famous names of the future such as George Bellows and Rockwell Kent. His most inspiring teacher was Robert Henri, who fostered in him a taste for subjects from everyday urban life in the USA, as well as a respect for the great realist masters of the past; Velázquez, Goya, Daumier, Manet and Degas.

In 1906-7, with the money he saved from a brief, unsatisfying stint of work as an illustrator with an advertising agency, and some help from his parents, Hopper was able to realize his ambition of visiting the art capital of the world, Paris. He stayed there for a few months and had an utterly un-bohemian time. His parents made arrangements through the Baptist Church for him to stay with a suitable bourgeois family, and he

The artist's mother
*(above) Elizabeth Griffiths Smith
Hopper encouraged her son's
talent for drawing. A devout
Baptist, she instilled in
Edward a taste for simplicity
and austerity, helping to
determine his decidedly
'puritanical' outlook.*

River birthplace
*(right) Edward was born in
Nyack, just above New York
City. The house, which his
grandfather had built in 1858,
overlooked the Hudson River,
where Edward developed his
love of boats.*

108

advertising agencies and strictly non-artistic journals such as *The Farmer's Wife, The Country Gentleman* and *System, the Magazine of Business*. On occasion, he would eke out his income by giving art lessons to children back home in Nyack, which he disliked even more. He managed to sell a painting for $250 at the famous Armory Show in 1913, and in 1918 won a prize of $300 from the US Shipping Board for a propaganda poster entitled *Smash the Hun,* but consistent success eluded him.

In 1913, Hopper took the studio at 3 Washington Square North in New York City that he occupied for the rest of his life, renting extra working and living space as his finances allowed, yet never altering the bare, spartan look of the place. The habit of thrift instilled in him by his upbringing and deepened by the lean early years of his career seems never to have left him, even after he became quite wealthy. He would eat in the shabbiest restaurants and diners, wear clothes until they were threadbare and buy second-hand

Robert Henri's class
(left) At the age of 18, Hopper enrolled at the New York School of Art, where he studied under the social realist painter, Robert Henri. This photo shows Hopper, third from the left, in the life-drawing class. Henri inspired such respect and devotion in his pupils, that he has been described as the 'silver-tongued Pied Piper'. His advice to them was to 'look at life around you'.

The Ashcan School
(below) Robert Henri (in the centre) was the leader of a group of painters whose vivid pictures of everyday life in New York – its streets and its tenements – earned them the title of the 'Ashcan' School. Hopper shared their commitment to objective realism, but he was not interested in their preoccupation with painting people or in their value of technical flair.

Key Dates

1882 born in Nyack, on the Hudson River

1900-6 attends New York School of Art, studying under Henri

1906-10 makes painting trips to Paris

1913 sells painting in Armory Show

1924 marries Jo Verstille Nivison; abandons commercial work

1932 shows work in Whitney Museum exhibition

1934 builds studio-house at Cape Cod

1950/64 retrospective exhibitions

1967 dies at studio in New York

seems to have taken no interest in avant-garde artists or their work. Instead, he came under the spell of Impressionism, and developed an interest in capturing effects of light that was to stay with him for his whole career as a painter. He was in Paris again in 1909 and 1910, after which he never again returned to Europe.

SLOW PROGRESS

Back in America, Hopper began to exhibit fairly regularly in New York, not at the conservative National Academy of Design, which rejected his work, but at the small anti-academic exhibitions organized by Robert Henri and other former pupils at the MacDowell Club. But no critics or collectors took any serious interest in him, and actually making a living from painting seemed out of the question. Indeed, it is a measure of the doggedness that was part of Hopper's character that he continued with art at all, only becoming a full-time painter in 1924, at the age of 42.

Until that date, Hopper reluctantly supported himself by commercial design and fairly routine illustrative jobs, working three days a week for

Smithsonian Institution, Washington

cars that he drove until they gave up the ghost.

Hopper had his first one-man exhibition in 1920, showing 16 oils painted in Paris and during summer trips to the bleak, rocky Monhegan Island, Maine, about 300 miles north-east of New York. Not a single work was sold, but the venue was an auspicious one – Whitney Studio Club. Founded by Gertrude Vanderbilt Whitney, this was the forerunner of the famous Whitney Museum of American Art. The museum was opened in 1931 and the same year bought *Early Sunday Morning* for its permanent collection. Hopper was to be closely associated with the Whitney throughout his life, showing new works in almost all the contemporary exhibitions that were held there from 1932 onwards.

SUCCESSFUL WATERCOLOURS

Unexpectedly, Hopper made his long-awaited breakthrough in watercolour rather than in oils. He only began using watercolour seriously in 1923, during a summer sketching trip to Gloucester, Massachusetts. Later that year, the Brooklyn Museum accepted six of the views he painted there for an exhibition; they were favourably noticed by reviewers and the museum bought one of them for $100. After a further successful watercolours' exhibition in 1924 at the gallery of Frank K. M. Rehn, who became his dealer for the rest of his life, Hopper at last felt sure enough of making a living to devote himself exclusively to painting.

On 9 July 1924, he married Josephine (Jo) Verstille Nivison at the Baptist 'Eglise Evangélique' in New York. They had been students together under Robert Henri and had met by chance on visits to Maine and Massachusetts. Jo had trained as an actress before she took up art, and was as talkative as Hopper was taciturn. She was tiny, had a strong character, hated domestic duties and

Commercial designs
(right) For many years, Hopper had to support himself by commercial art, working part-time as an illustrator in an advertising agency and producing posters and illustrations – often humorous – for various magazines and business journals. He had no trouble getting his work published and won a prize of $300 for one of his wartime propaganda posters; but he later said, 'I was a rotten illustrator – or mediocre anyway.'

Work in advertising
(below) This photograph shows Hopper in 1906 (seated right foreground) at work in the advertising agency of C. C. Phillips & Co. Hopper always looked back on his commercial career with some bitterness, although his period with Coles Phillips (seen working opposite him) earned him enough money to finance his painting trips to Paris.

Whitney Museum of American Art, New York

loved cats. Jo was also possessive, and insisted that Hopper gave up drawing from the nude model unless she modelled for him. As a result, many of the women in his paintings, and all the nudes, are portraits of Jo.

It was in the mid-1920s that Hopper forged the very distinctive style that we associate with his name, and his work changed little from then on. The growing reputation he enjoyed was reflected in the increasingly prestigious exhibitions devoted to him: a one-man show at the Frank K. M. Rehn Gallery in 1929, retrospectives at the Museum of Modern Art in 1933 and the Whitney Museum in

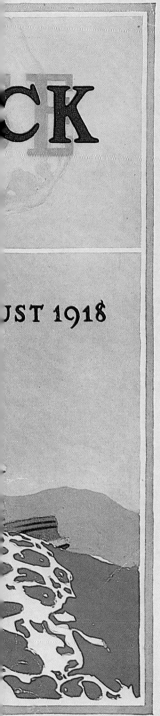

JST 1918

Josephine N. Hopper Bequest/Geoffrey Clements

Whitney Museum of American Art, New York

Marriage to Jo

(above) In July 1924, Hopper married Josephine (Jo) Verstille Nivison, an artist who had also studied under Robert Henri. Hopper met her when he returned to the school for a visit and had helped her stretch her canvas. Jo was Hopper's ideal companion; she shared his frugal tastes, had a keen sense of humour, and loved country life. She was a vivacious as Hopper was dour: she once described 'talking with Eddie' as 'just like dropping a stone in a well, except that it doesn't thump when it hits bottom'.

1950, and a major retrospective at the Whitney in 1964 which toured afterwards to the Art Institute of Chicago, the Detroit Institute of Arts and the City Art Museum of St Louis.

Hopper also accumulated prizes and honours. In 1932, the National Academy of Design elected him an associate member, which he was pleased to refuse – as the Academy had refused him during his years of struggle and obscurity. The Pennsylvania Academy of the Fine Arts awarded him the Temple Gold Medal in 1935, the first of many such awards from American academies and museums. He won a series of prizes at the Art

Institute of Chicago, which in 1950 conferred upon him the honorary degree of Doctor of Fine Arts; he was one of the four artists chosen to represent the USA at the Venice Biennale of 1952; and in 1955, the American Academy of Arts and Letters presented him with a Gold Medal for Painting.

By 1934, Hopper was able to build a studio-home away from it all at South Truro on Cape Cod, where he and Jo stayed for part of almost every summer for the rest of their lives. Success also enabled him to indulge his liking for travel – it is no accident that so many of Hopper's paintings depict hotels, motels and life on the road – and in 1941, he and Jo made a three-month grand tour by car across the country to the West Coast and back. In 1943, there was a petrol shortage that prevented them from driving anywhere, even up to Cape Cod, so they made a train trip to Mexico instead, the first of a number of holidays they spent there.

Hopper's pleasures in life were never extravagant. He enjoyed the theatre, the cinema and books. He was quite exceptionally well read – and not only in English literature: he was able to quote fluently from Goethe and the French Symbolist poets in the original. He was especially

The Armory Show

The modern movement in art burst upon the American scene in 1913 with a huge exhibition which came to be known as the Armory Show. It was held in New York in the newly-built premises of the 69th Infantry Regiment, and attracted about 70,000 visitors. Strong feelings were aroused by the more avant-garde Europeans, like Matisse and Duchamp, but Hopper managed to sell his first painting.

The Red Studio (1911)
(below) Matisse was particularly well-represented in the show and his work was lampooned by the press. He was dismissed as an 'apostle of ugliness' and his work as 'unbelievable childishness'.

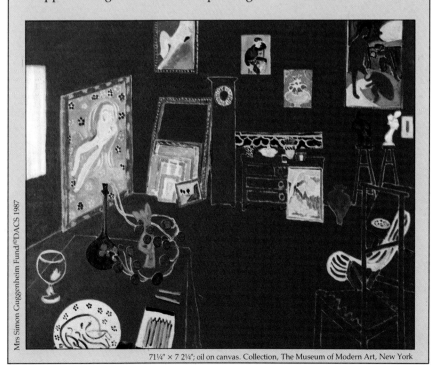

Mrs Simon Guggenheim Fund/©DACS 1987

71¼" × 7 2¼"; oil on canvas. Collection, The Museum of Modern Art, New York

fond of Symbolist verse, first discovering it as a student and as late as 1951, giving Jo a volume of Rimbaud for Christmas with an affectionate inscription in French. Indeed, there is a strange melancholy about many of his paintings that the Symbolists, and most of all Baudelaire, would surely have recognized.

A SELF-MADE MAN

In spite of his rather sophisticated literary tastes, Hopper cultivated the public persona of the down-to-earth self-made man who cared little for fancy ideas. This may well have been a ploy designed to exempt him from seriously discussing his own work. When interviewed, he usually refused to acknowledge any intellectual or personal content in his pictures and claimed to be merely working within the American Realist tradition, painting neither more nor less than what he happened to see around him.

Hopper was also wholly committed to representational art and watched the rise of Abstract Expressionist painting in the 1950s and 60s with dismay. He was a member of the group of representational painters who, in 1953, launched the journal *Reality* as a mouthpiece for their point of view, serving for a time on its editorial committee. In 1960, he and his *Reality* colleagues made a concerted protest to the Whitney Museum

Washington Square
(right) In 1913, Hopper moved to 3 Washington Square North, where he continued to live after his marriage. He divided his studio in half – so that Jo had an equal space to paint in – and later they spent the long summer months away at Cape Cod.

Detailed record
(below) Hopper and his wife kept a catalogue of all the oils, watercolours and prints that he exhibited or sold in his lifetime. Every picture was illustrated and accompanied by detailed notes, describing the subject-matter, the colours, the buyer and even the purchase price.

Norman Tomalin/Bruce Coleman Ltd.

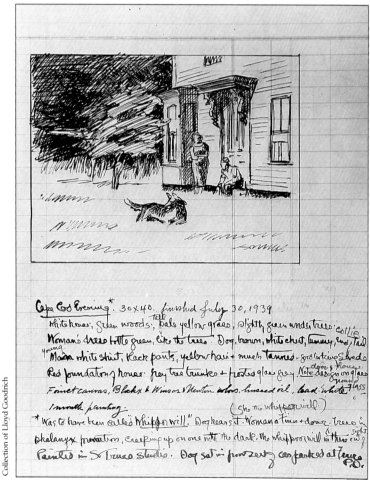

Collection of Lloyd Goodrich

Cape Cod Evening/Whitney Museum of American Art, New York

Summers at Cape Cod

Cape Cod is a long finger of land curving out into the Atlantic about 250 miles along the coast from New York. Since the 19th century it has been famous for its spectacular scenery and for the summer colony of artists who gather at the very tip of the peninsula in Provincetown. Typically, Hopper shunned Provincetown in favour of the sleepier community of South Truro. Here he rented 'Bird Cage Cottage' during the summers of 1930-33, and in 1934 built a simple studio-house to his own designs. After this, Hopper and his wife spent almost every summer at Cape Cod for the rest of their lives.

High road

(right) This watercolour of 1931, made during a summer of Cape Cod, shows a sweep of empty road lined by houses in the clear light of late afternoon. Hopper once said; 'There's something soft about Cape Cod that doesn't appeal to me too much. But there's a beautiful light there – very luminous – perhaps because it's so far out to sea: an island almost.'

Bequest of Josephine N. Hopper/Geoffrey Clements

and the Museum of Modern Art against the 'gobbledegook influences' of abstract art in their collections. Curiously enough, the abstract painters expressed nothing but admiration for Hopper, in whose work they saw an interest in pure form and a play of space against flatness that anticipated their own experiments.

In the words of one friend, Hopper gave off 'a sense of geological presence that redefined inertia'. He was slow and laconic in his work as a painter, completing only two or three oils a year, and even more so in his social manner. He regarded conversation as mere chatter, not worth the physical effort required to produce it. If he had nothing to say, which was generally the case, he would remain silent. The idea of filling in awkward moments with small talk would have seemed as absurd to him as filling in the empty wall-surfaces in his paintings with pretty decorations.

CHERISHED PRIVACY

Critics inferred from the lonely mood that pervades so many of Hopper's paintings that he must himself have suffered loneliness. He certainly spent much of his time alone, whether painting, reading or deep in thought, but it was by choice. He cherished solitude and had little love of company except that of his wife. The unsmiling, suspicious look on his face in photographs makes

Hans Namuth

Last years
(above) The fame that Hopper achieved in his late years made little impression on his and Jo's personal lives. They continued to live simply, dividing their time between the city and countryside, and painting at a leisurely pace. In 1967, Hopper fell ill, and on 15 May he died in his studio in Washington Square North.

us feel that we have intruded into a very private life. It also, somehow, makes us feel small. Hopper's withdrawal from the world was rooted in a profound pessimism; the same friend wrote that 'he views his fellow man as a flimsy and often trivial construct'.

The word that invariably crops up in the recollections of those who knew Hopper is 'puritan'. He did come from an Anglo-Saxon Protestant background: his parents were of Dutch and English origins, and both devout Baptists. More significantly, he always conveyed the impression of strong feelings kept tightly under control, despising any kind of self-indulgent emotionalism or ostentation – as though to give so much away made a person ridiculous.

In 1965, Hopper painted his last picture, *Two Comedians*, showing a couple reminiscent of himself and Jo taking their final bow before leaving the stage. He died in his studio at 3 Washington Square North on 15 May 1967, aged 84. Jo died the following year and bequeathed the entire artistic estate, including over 2,000 of Hopper's paintings, watercolours, drawings and prints, to the Whitney Museum of American Art.

Whitney Museum of American Art, New York

Silence and Solitariness

Hopper's highly original work gives us an uneasy view of modern life in America, stressing in particular the loneliness and isolation of man in the urban environment.

House by the Railroad (1925). 24" × 29"; oil on canvas

Collection, The Museum of Modern Art, New York. Given anonymously

harsh, seeming to condemn the garishness of modern taste.

Hopper disliked being pigeon-holed as a painter of 'the American scene' – there seemed something patronizing about it. Yet the modern life he depicts is unmistakably and insistently modern life in the USA. Hopper's great strength was his eye for a good subject, and what better subject for a painter of modernity than a New World, the discordant grandeur of which had virtually never been exploited in art?

Though Hopper is best known as an oil painter, some of his most important early work was in watercolour and etching. He first won recognition as a painter with the daintily executed, sunlight-filled watercolours he made in Gloucester,

Hugo Kastor Fund 1962

By temperament and by training, Hopper was a realist. Following in the aesthetic tradition developed by Manet, Degas and the Impressionists in the nineteenth century, he had no time for idealization, prettification or fantasy – he had no time for beauty, in the conventional sense of that word. His aim was to recreate the experience of reality intensely perceived, showing us the kind of people, places and things that we might see every day, yet somehow imbuing them with that strange and elusive quality we usually, for want of a preciser term, call 'mood'.

At his best, Hopper was a painter of modernity – he delighted in representing those things that make modern life modern, from petrol stations to cafeterias. His main province is the public place; private life is only glimpsed through windows, in doorways, at a distance. He presents a detached view, as if observing modern man for the purposes of some behaviour study. His brushwork is slow, deliberate and dull, like the most deadpan of commentaries, and his colour can be almost cruelly

House by the Railroad
(above) Having experimented with prints, Hopper returned to oils in 1920, but with new vision. This culminated in House by the Railroad *– a bold rendering of a fantastic house cut off by railway tracks, utterly alone in an empty landscape.*

Lighthouse at Two Lights
(right) Hopper produced many watercolours in the 1920s. Cape Elizabeth, Maine, was known for its spectacular surf, but here Hopper chose to portray the lighthouse.

Whitney Museum of American Art, New York

Massachusetts in 1923, and he continued to use the medium with a relaxed, lively touch throughout his life. The black-and-white technique of etching lent itself more readily than watercolour to representing the seamy side of the American scene, and Hopper's etchings of the early 1920s dwell upon landscapes cut across by railway tracks and life in cheap apartment blocks. It was here that we see his peculiar brand of realism beginning to emerge.

THE INHUMANITY OF THE MANMADE

One of the leading ideas in Hopper's work is the inhumanity of the manmade. He can suggest the hugeness and bleakness of a big city by showing just a street corner or the view from a train window. Architectural forms take on a strange alien presence, mean, hard and repetitive in the city, aggressively ornate in the suburbs and small towns. Sometimes the environment is allowed to speak for itself, like a stage-set without actors. Elsewhere there are people, but they are somehow temporary; they seem not really to inhabit the place where they happen to be.

The principal legacy of Hopper's Paris days, when he saw and imitated the work of the

The artist's etchings
(above) Hopper began etching in 1915 and this was the medium in which he first expressed his view of modern America. Evening Wind (1921) realistically portrays a hot summer night in the city and gives us a theme which is to recur in his work – the nude in a city interior.

Shoshone Cliffs (1941)
(below) Hopper painted the country as much as the city and in landscape responded to the natural formations of cliffs, boulders and sand dunes. He wrote, 'My aim in painting has always been the most exact transcription possible of my most intimate impressions of nature'.

The Metropolitan Museum of Art, New York

The Butler Institute of American Art, Youngstown, Ohio

Impressionists, was an abiding interest in the play of light and shade on objects, especially the effects of sunlight on buildings, inside and out. Hopper orchestrates light as ingeniously as any lighting manager in the theatre, and the shadows and areas of light take on as much of a life of their own as the figures and objects over which they play. Indeed, they perform the crucial function of enlivening and competing with the those figures and objects.

The angles from which Hopper's subjects are viewed may look casually chosen, even accidental. He will sometimes crop a scene so that a figure is cut in half, sometimes show the main figure to one side as if by mistake, allowing most of the composition to be taken up with something ostensibly rather boring. But these are calculated and essential effects, often to emphasise a sense of alienation. Photographs might also play a part in the process, although the image is always quite transformed in the final painting.

Another of Hopper's recurrent themes is

Empty Spaces

In his paintings, Hopper is the master of the empty space. His near-empty rooms illustrate the starkness of modern life, without personal detail to provide emotional comfort. He also used space to represent the psychological distance between people.

Bequest of Stephen Carlton Clark

detail: Western Motel/Yale University Art Gallery, New Haven

Interior Scenes

Artists have often used interior settings to enhance the meaning of their works. The Victorians, for instance, were particularly fond of pictures that told a story, preferably moral, and domestic interiors often proved the perfect setting. Artistic devices were used to create certain effects, such as indoor light and details of furnishings which made interior scenes seem real and familiar – they also tell us a great deal about the taste and spirit of the time. The use of viewpoints that would give a casual through-the-keyhole quality were explored, and artists also used the space between figures to suggest either their closeness or the psychological distance between them.

The Curtis Publishing Co., Indianapolis, Indiana

Reprinted from The Saturday Evening Post c.1950

Tate Gallery, London

Norman Rockwell (1894-1978) **Shuffleton's Barber Shop** *(above) Rockwell was a chronicler of everyday America. When painting this picture of the barbers enjoying their time off, he worked from photographs.*

Sir W. Q. Orchardson (1835-1910) **The First Cloud** *This Scottish painter specialized in scenes of upper-class marital tension, as in this painting of the first quarrel.*

transience. His scenes of travel carry implications that transcend the modern-life context – they stand in an age-old poetic tradition in which the journey is used to suggest man's journey through life. The roads and railways in Hopper's paintings, the travellers sitting on trains or waiting for who knows what in hotel rooms and lobbies, are images of human existence as a transient thing, images of mortality.

The people in his work often seem to be in a world of their own, gazing dreamily into space or intently reading. Sometimes the parts of the setting around their heads or in front of their eyes will seem to contain their hovering thoughts, but there is rarely any sense of communication between them. Instead, they tend to be divided from one another by the furniture or the architecture into separate compartments of space. They are not brought together by any definite storyline either. Despite his training as an illustrator, Hopper deliberately avoids narrative

Office at Night (1940)
(below and detail right)
All the themes for which Hopper is famous are here in this painting of an office at night glimpsed through a window, where there is no communication between the two people. The composition is viewed from above looking down and based on diagonals, the cool overhead light contrasting with the warm light from the window. The woman (detail) seems to wait interminably for some sign from her boss, at the same time absorbed in a world of her own.

Walker Art Centre, Minneapolis

Gift of the T. B. Walker Foundation/Gilbert M. Walker Fund 1948

content in his works. Something is going on but there is no way of telling what, and the situation is all the more fascinating for its ambiguity.

Hopper was above all a master of expressive space and, in a way, the spaces between the figures are more important than the figures themselves. The world he creates in his paintings seems to yawn with emptiness. Most obviously, he will use empty seats to suggest absence, imparting a lonely and isolated air to the people who are present. More subtly, his compositions are contrived to make us look for something that is not there, to give an uneasy feeling of watching and waiting for someone to arrive, or some event to occur. To increase our unease, he will slightly distort perspective, just enough for us to sense that something is wrong without being able to say exactly what it is. He was a realist, but with an angle, and his aims and methods were hardly as straightforward as that term might imply.

117

THE MAKING OF A MASTERPIECE

Nighthawks

Hopper's lonely streets become even lonelier at night, the empty space all the more disquieting for being filled with darkness. He once said that if he created an effect of strange isolation in *Nighthawks*, it was 'unconsciously' and not by design. The nighthawks take temporary refuge in a cheap diner on a deserted, anonymous corner in New York. They drink coffee in the dead of night as if to combat sleep, as if they had no homes to go to. The hands of the couple almost touch, yet they neither look at each other nor talk – there is an uncertain promise of sex, but none of real communication. *Nighthawks* is Hopper's best-known work, probably because it seems so completely to embody the spirit of the time at which it was painted. Like the subjects in *Nighthawks*, Americans in 1942 could look along two dark streets: a past full of grim memories of the Great Depression, and a future blackened by the spectacle of World War II.

> 'The only real influence
> I've ever had was myself.'
>
> Edward Hopper

In the shadows
(left) The focus of the picture is on the couple and the attendant, but this figure, on the left, balances the composition. The fact that we cannot see his face because his back is turned and that he keeps himself apart from the others in half shadow adds a slightly menacing note to the mood of the painting.

The couple
(right) Because the couple are sitting together and are almost touching, we assume they are together. But each seems self-absorbed, there is no communication between them. Hopper's theme of isolation is amply in evidence.

The Art Institute of Chicago

Whitney Museum of American Art, New York

The wedge
(above) Hopper's sketch shows the structure on which his composition is based. The shape of the restaurant is a wedge thrusting into the picture, and countered by the solid row of shops.

Preliminary sketches
(right) Here Hopper is working out the details of the arms and hands of the man and woman, which in the final painting are exactly the same. The girl's expression and neckline, however, have changed.

Whitney Museum of American Art, New York

Gallery

Hopper came late to artistic maturity and
once he had formed his distinctive style, it
changed little. He seized on a visual world
that no one before him had seriously
explored and made it definitively his own. It
is the world of modern America – of concrete
and glass, of motels and filling stations,
and poignant emptiness amid abundance.

John Tennant

Eleven a.m. *1926*
28″ × 36″ Hirshhorn Museum and Sculpture Garden,
Smithsonian Institution, Washington

*The central theme of Hopper's work is the spiritual emptiness of
modern urban life, and here he shows a woman staring listlessly out of
her window at another uneventful day. Her facial expression is not
shown, but Hopper masterfully conveys her weariness through the
sluggish attitude of her body. Although his work is in many ways
austere, Hopper was extremely frank in his depiction of the nude, and
the figure here has a very solid sense of physical presence, in keeping
with the firmness of structure of the picture as a whole.*

120

From this stagnancy, however, Hopper extracted freshness, painting with utter directness and sureness of hand. The economy of his style reflects the frugality of his life: nothing is overemphasized, there are no unnecessary details and no virtuosity. Generally he limits himself to one or two figures in a spare setting (Nighthawks has an unusually large cast). There is no overt social comment and no attempt to tell a story, and although Hopper's pictures vividly reflect the time and the place in which he lived, there is nothing parochial about them. In their depiction of the isolation of individuals, they strike emotional chords that are easily recognizable today.

Automat *1927*
28″ × 36″ Des Moines Art Center, Iowa

Hopper was a very careful and deliberate worker and he had an uncanny gift for achieving a perfect balance between figure and setting; the setting is never simply a background for some action and his figures are never just animating details in an urban landscape. Here the single quiet figure is unerringly placed in her commonplace surroundings, and her troubled isolation, as she contemplates her life over a cup of coffee, comes over with great immediacy. As always with Hopper, all the details ring true and he achieves his goal naturally, without any striving for effect.

Early Sunday Morning *1930*
35″ × 60″ Whitney Museum of
American Art, New York

*The inspiration for this picture
probably came from a stage set for the
play* Street Scene *by Elmer Rice,
which Hopper saw in New York in
1929. Like the picture, the set
featured a rather bleak two-storey
block seen flat on and stretching the
entire width of the stage. Hopper
found architecture a very appealing
subject, as it gave him the clarity and
firmness of line he loved. Here he
needs no human presence to create a
sense of pictorial drama, relying
instead on the bold forms and
the morning light.*

Geoffrey Clements

26¼″ × 40¼″, oil on canvas. Collection, The Museum of Modern Art, New York. Mrs. Simon Guggenheim Fund

Gas *(1940)*
26¼″ × 40¼″ Museum of
Modern Art, New York

*Hopper liked to go driving when
he was looking for inspiration,
and subjects drawn from the
highway figure prominently in
his work. This is perhaps the
most striking of them all, vividly
suggesting the anxious sense of
isolation that a lonely road can
bring as night falls. Hopper did
not depict a specific site here, but
put together a synthesis in the
studio from sketches he had made
at various places.*

Nighthawks *1942*
33¼″ × 60⅛″ Art Institue of
Chicago

*Hopper's most famous painting
was 'suggested by a restaurant
on Greenwich Avenue where
two streets meet'. Although he
hated discussing his work,
Hopper was a little more
forthcoming than usual about
this picture: 'Nighthawks
seems to be the way I think of a
night street. I didn't see it as
particularly lonely. I simplified
the scene a great deal and made
the restaurant bigger.
Unconsciously, perhaps, I was
painting the loneliness of a
large city.'*

Friends of American Art 1942.51/© Art Institute of Chicago. All rights reserved.

126

Western Motel *1957*
30¼″ × 50⅛″ Yale University
Art Gallery, New Haven

*Appropriately for someone who
enjoyed travelling so much,
hotel rooms and lobbies were
favourite subjects of Hopper's.
The soullessness of the
surroundings and the boredom
and frustration of waiting
provided him with ideal subject
matter. Here he also conveys a
feeling of tension, suggested by
the woman's expression and
rigid pose, but as usual he makes
nothing explicit.*

Sunlight in a Cafeteria 1958
40¼" × 60⅛" Yale University Art Gallery, New Haven

The figures in Hopper's paintings rarely communicate directly with one another, and here he brilliantly depicts a feeling of hesitancy. The man looks vacantly towards the window, but his thoughts are surely on the girl, while she sits fidgeting with her hands.

Second-Storey Sunlight 1960
40″ × 50″ Whitney Museum of American Art, New York

In his usual self-effacing way, Hopper said this picture was only 'an attempt to paint sunlight as white with almost no yellow pigment in the white. Any psychological idea will have to be supplied by the viewer.'

Geoffrey Clements

The Ashcan School

Labelled as vulgar by the critics, the Ashcan school of painters was a flourishing and original group whose inspiration was drawn from New York street scenes and the seamier side of city life.

In the early years of the 20th century, American painting finally emerged from the shadow of European art and began to assert its own identity. Leading these advances was a group of social realist painters who came to be known as the Ashcan school.

The leader of this influential group was the painter and teacher Robert Henri. Born Robert Henry Cozad, Henri changed his name after his family was forced to flee Cincinnati following his father's involvement in a shooting incident. Henri's own work came firmly within the European orbit, his portraits bearing a close resemblance to those of Manet. However, Henri's true importance lay in the direction that his teaching gave to the realist movement. One

Street Scene with Snow
(below) Robert Henri became the founder of the anti-academic Ashcan school. The new realistic trend was not shy in seeking its inspiration from all aspects of American city life. But, nevertheless, European influence remained strong. Henri's debt to Manet can be seen in his brushwork, which captures the immediacy of a scene.

Yale University Art Gallery

commentator described him as a 'silver-tongued Pied Piper'.

Henri travelled to Europe on several occasions in the 1880s and 1890s. In 1888, he was in Paris, studying under the academic painter, Adolphe Bouguereau and, in 1895, he visited Holland with William Glackens. Like Henri, Glackens' link with the Ashcan school was tempered by his obvious fondness for European art and his canvases reveal a particular liking for the work of Renoir.

On his return to the States, Henri settled in Philadelphia and, from 1892-95, he taught at the Women's School of Design. His own studio became a popular meeting place for artists and it was during this period that the future members of the Ashcan school first came together. Many of these artists worked initially as illustrators on newspapers. George Luks, Everett Shinn, John Sloan and William Glackens all began their careers

Addison Gallery of American Art/Phillips Academy Andover, Massachusetts

Sunday, Women Drying their Hair

(left) John Sloan chose not to portray the moneyed classes popular with the 'genteel tradition' at the turn of the last century, but the unpretentious, yet picturesque, lower-middle class life of back-street New York.

audiences and street scenes in the slums were typical subjects, while bars like McSorleys provided a virtual replica of night life in the Latin Quarter of Paris.

In New York, however, they also came up against the opposition of the National Academy of Design. This imposing body had been founded in 1826 and was, in its early days, an important sponsor of native American art. By the time that Impressionism and Realism made their appearance, however, it had become extremely conservative. In 1907, Luks, Glackens and Shinn were among the artists who had their works rejected for its annual show. Henri, who was one of the selection committee on this occasion, withdrew his own entries in protest and set about organizing an independent exhibition.

The result was a show by 'the Eight', which took place in February 1908 at the Macbeth Galleries, where Henri had previously held a one-man exhibition. 'The Eight' were not a cohesive group and this was to be the only time they exhibited together. Nonetheless, the vitality and modernity of the paintings on display made this a landmark of American art and a rallying point for supporters of the avant-garde. The critics,

this way, before Henri persuaded them to take up painting and translate the immediacy and topicality of their journalistic work into a vigorous new form of American art.

Henri preached a positive brand of liberal humanism, stressing his belief in progress, justice and the common bonds of humanity. He called upon artists to portray modern American life, not with the superficial prettiness that was popular in the academies, but with the social awareness of a Goya or a Daumier. 'Be willing to paint a picture that does not look like a picture,' was his maxim.

ACADEMIC REJECTION

Towards the end of the 19th century, the Philadelphia realist painters migrated to New York, where the overcrowded suburbs gave an increasingly urban slant to their pictures. Cinema

Hammerstein's Roof Garden

(right) William James Glackens was probably the most gifted, if conservative, of that group of artists who matured in Philadelphia at the end of the last century. Glackens, like Sloan, worked as a newspaper illustrator before moving to New York. Though his subject matter is very much urban, he was more preoccupied with form and colour than with content.

Geoffrey Clements

Whitney Museum of American Art, New York

he singled out the former's *Night Windows* for particular praise. Then, a year later, he produced his own version, using the same voyeuristic theme of a woman glimpsed through an open window.

Where Sloan viewed the life of the poor with sympathy and as a forum for political struggle, George Luks found the slums a source of vigour, excitement and modernity. Luks, himself, was a flamboyant and brash character and sought to project this image in a series of extravagant fabrications about his early career. His claims to have earned a living as a coal miner and as a fighter called 'Chicago Whitey' and 'the Harlem Spider' are probably apocryphal, but it is true that he was almost killed by a firing squad when, as a reporter, he was sent to cover the Spanish-American war in Cuba. Luks' painting shows a similar sense of adventure, with a loose handling and brushwork that reveals a clear debt to Frans Hals. His style is best exemplified by his depiction of wrestlers.

RED-BLOODED ART

Fighting scenes were also popular with George Bellows, another painter associated with the Ashcan school. Bellows did not exhibit with 'the Eight', but his art contained many of the aggressively American qualities that typified the spirit of the group. He never went abroad and thus found it easier than his colleagues to ward off European influences. In addition, he was a keen sportsman and seemed to symbolize the Ashcan ideal of the all-American, red-blooded male.

In his youth, he played semi-pro baseball at Columbus, Ohio, and was invited to join the

Woman's Work (c.1911)
(above) Sloan was very much interested in genre scenes, often seen from his studio window. His work on a newspaper had given him speed in drawing and a reporter's eye. He also had an almost photographic memory and tended to regard illustration as his true métier. Though a close friend and student of Henri, he rejected his teacher's virtuosity for a more thoughtful approach – as reflected in his tranquil paintings.

however, were less enthusiastic. 'Vulgarity smites one in the face at this exhibition,' complained one correspondent, and the feeling that certain artists were glorying in the noise and the squalor of city life earned them the tag of 'the Ashcan school'.

Only five of 'the Eight' were attached to the Ashcan group – Henri, Luks, Shinn, Sloan and Glackens. Of these, probably the artist who best typified its spirit was John Sloan, who is sometimes known as 'the American Hogarth'. Sloan was a committed socialist and was later a co-founder of *The Masses*, a political journal to which Henri, Luks and Bellows all contributed illustrations. His diaries show how closely he based his paintings on the scenes and incidents that he witnessed in the city streets. Hopper was a fervent admirer of his work and in an article of 1927, entitled 'John Sloan and the Philadelphians',

The Miner (1925)

(right) George Luks grew up in a mining community in Pennsylvania. Once an artist-reporter, he did not eschew portraying the less pleasant aspects of working life; and his painting, The Miner, *is not just direct reporting – more a social comment. Exhausted after a filthy day down the shaft, the miner stares disconcertingly at the comfortable viewer.*

Stag at Sharkey's (1907)

This painting of an illegal boxing match by George Bellows, once an athlete himself, was hailed as a 'landmark of realism'. It conveys all the movement and excitement of both spectators and combatants intent on drawing blood. Bellows is said to have remarked when criticized for pugilistic inaccuracy, 'I don't know anything about boxing. I am just painting two men trying to kill each other.'

National Gallery of Art, Washington

Chester Dale Collection

Cincinnati Reds. Bellows chose art as a career instead, although his continuing interest in sport is evident from his paintings. He depicted baseball, polo and tennis scenes, but is most famous for six stirring pictures of boxing matches.

Prize-fighting was illegal in New York at this time, and bouts were staged in private athletic clubs, with both the spectators and the fighters taking out temporary membership. Bellows' studio was almost opposite Sharkey's Club in Broadway, and this venue provided a rich source of material for him. His brutal ringside views are remarkable both for the blurred, mask-like faces of the audience and for their sheer presence which, in the absence of photographic reporting, must have seemed all the more striking. Bellows emphasised his interest in the physicality of such scenes. 'Who cares what a prize-fighter looks like?' he

commented, 'It's muscles that count.'

Bellows had considerable conventional success, becoming the youngest Associate of the National Academy in 1909. For his colleagues, however, it was more important to set an alternative standard to these academic plaudits. In 1910, Henri organized the Exhibition of Independent Artists; it was the first American show to have no jury and no prizes, and where each painter paid for the space he used.

Three years later, modern art made its decisive breakthrough in America at the Armory Show. Ironically, the impact of the European contributions at this exhibition made the work of the urban realists seem old-fashioned and heralded their decline. It required the emergence of Hopper, Henri's pupil, to underline the true achievements of the Ashcan school.

A Year in 1929
the Life

Hopper had already forged his distinctive style so evocative of urban desolation when the Wall Street Crash of 1929 shattered the American Boom and international hopes for peace and prosperity. A world depression and the 'Hungry Thirties' were just around the corner.

For most of 1929, the Western world was not only prosperous but peaceful. One government after another committed its people to the 1928 Kellogg-Briand Pact which renounced war as an instrument of policy. The USSR and USA, though non-members of the League of Nations, adhered to the Pact, which eventually had 65 signatories. In 1929, the Young Plan tackled the remaining cause of ill-feeling between Germany and the wartime Allies by slashing the burden of reparations, and Allied troops began evacuating the Rhineland, which had been occupied since the end of the War. The French statesman Aristide Briand put forward proposals for a federated Europe.

A spate of books appeared which were more or less openly anti-war, concentrating on its horrors rather than questions of national 'war guilt'. Three famous examples, published in 1929,

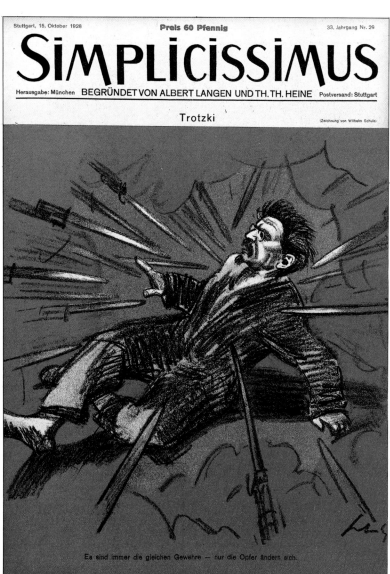

Trotsky under attack
(above) Trotsky's brilliant oratory and tireless energy in the service of the Revolution had made him appear the obvious successor to Lenin, but he had reckoned without Stalin's gradual accumulation of power. Moreover, the split between Stalin's opportunistic backing of soviet socialism and Trotsky's call for 'Permanent Revolution' formed the ideological premise for Trotsky's expulsion from the Party in 1927 and his exile in 1929.

Jean-Loup Charmet

were Robert Graves's autobiography *Goodbye To All That*, Ernest Hemingway's *A Farewell to Arms*, and the German writer Erich Maria Remarque's international best-seller – later a famous film – *All Quiet on the Western Front*.

THE WALL STREET CRASH

The economic situation in the West was somewhat shaken except in the United States, where real wages and national wealth had doubled since the War. Prices of shares soared on the Wall Street Stock Exchange, till it seemed that, if you bought, you were certain to make money. Speculative mania raised the Dow Jones index to 300 by the end of 1928, and the trend continued through 1929. The index peaked at 381 in August 1929; then, in September, confidence faltered and on 'Black Thursday', 24 October, the Crash came, with wave after wave of panic selling. By November, Dow Jones was down to 197 and thousands of speculators had been ruined. Frightened people rushed to secure their remaining capital, causing a disastrous run on the banks followed by closures that created new panics. In a downward spiral, industries were disrupted and millions became unemployed. The Great Depression lasted for years and, since the USA was a great creditor nation (and was soon to start calling in its loans), it spread all over the industrialized world. Apart from shattering the European economies, the Depression wrecked the Young Plan, destroyed many people's faith in democracy, and made possible the rise of Hitler and other dictators.

Disaster on Wall Street

(left) The first hint that all was not well in the American stock market occurred on Saturday, 19 October 1929. The market, fed by an artificial boom, had been spiralling madly since June when rumours of governmental stringency led to a wave of selling which escalated in the week to follow. The intervention of the big banks after Black Thursday (24 October) only temporarily revived a market which continued to sell in panic. It was not long before the Depression was felt not only throughout America but also by her trading partners in Europe; between 1929 and 1933 the volume of world trade shrank by two-thirds.

Giancarlo Costa

Walter Rawlings/Robert Harding Picture Library

Villa Savoie

(above) The Swiss architect Charles-Edouard Jeanneret, more commonly known as Le Corbusier, had already established an international reputation by the time he began work on the Villa Savoie in Poissy, France (1928-30). Perhaps his most famous house, it illustrates his new unfettered approach using reinforced concrete. In complete contrast to traditional design, the house is raised on columns with a roof garden, room size is no longer dependant on load-bearing walls and windows run the length of the equally freed façade.

King of crime

(left) Al Capone, the almost legendary gangster boss of Chicago, lorded over a vice empire based on the sale of illegal liquor during the Prohibition years. An Italian by birth, Capone had imported the techniques of the Sicilian Mafia to establish a bootleg monopoly and crush all opposition. Armour-plated cars and machine guns were soon familiar sights on Chicago streets of the late Twenties. The high point of his vicious career was the St Valentine's Day Massacre of 1929, in which the entire Bugs Moran gang were mown down by machine-gun.

The Bettmann Archive/BBC Hulton Picture Library

This year also marked the beginning of a new era for Soviet Russia, where Joseph Stalin had emerged as the leading figure. Stalin's principal rival, Trotsky, went into exile, and his theory of fomenting world-wide 'permanent revolution' was abandoned in favour of Stalin's policy of building 'socialism in one country'. At the same time Stalin defeated the 'Right Opposition', which opposed as premature the policy of collectivizing agriculture. The Rightist leader, Bukharin, and his closest associates were expelled from the Politburo.

Other events of 1929 included Alexander, King of the Serbs, Croats and Slovenes, declaring himself dictator, and re-naming his kingdom Yugoslavia. As a result of the Lateran Treaties between the Papacy and Mussolini's Italy, the Pope ceased to be the 'prisoner of the Vatican' (self-immured since the new Italian state seized the city of Rome in 1870). The Vatican was recognized as an independent city-state and Catholicism became in effect the state religion.

In 1929, the 'Talkies' were all the rage, and cinemas everywhere were being re-wired for sound. Sunbathing had become popular, and the first precautionary aids — sun-tan lotion and Mexican straw hats — appeared. The German *Graf Zeppelin* airship flew around the world while Richard Byrd, the American pioneer aviator, flew over the South Pole. The Museum of Modern Art in New York was opened. The ballet impresario Serge Diaghilev died, as did the two giants of First World War France, Marshal Foch and George Clemenceau. More ominously, so did the architect of Franco-German reconciliation, Gustav Stresemann.

Bundespost Museum, Frankfurt

The Graf Zeppelin

(left) This celebrated rigid airship, built in 1928, was piloted by Hugo Eckener on a round the world trip the following year. The 21,255 mile flight was completed in 20 days, 4 hours and 14 minutes. This painting of the Graf Zeppelin *shows the airship on a regular flight in 1931, one of the many during nine years of service.*

Les Enfants Terribles

(right) Jean Cocteau (1889-1963) was himself an enfant terrible *of the Twenties and Thirties, dazzling the cultural milieu of Paris and beyond with his versatile genius, applied not only to every literary genre but also in the worlds of art, music and the cinema. His avowed aim as an artist was to 'throw a bomb' to shock, dazzle and amuse. His great novel* Les Enfants Terribles *(1929) succeeds perfectly. It evokes the world view of four adolescents who exist in an intense and unreal world of their own creation.*

Collection Laosat/Explorer Archives © DACS 1987

Kobal Collection

Pandora's Box

(above) This compelling silent film, based on two plays by the German Frank Wedekind, charts the rise and fall of Lulu, a latter-day Circe, whose beauty enchants while her amorality leads her and those who love her to destruction. The director, G. W. Pabst, had no reason to regret his choice of the American Louise Brooks to play Lulu. A natural actress, she brought to the role a charismatic blend of innocence and seduction to create one of the most memorable screen performances.

GALLERY GUIDE

Whistler

The two major holdings of Whistler's work are in Washington (Freer Gallery) and in Glasgow (Hunterian Art Gallery and the Burrell Collection). The former owns The Peacock Room (p.36) and several oriental works, while the National Gallery of Art (also in Washington) possesses *The White Girl*. In London, the Tate Gallery houses a number of the Nocturnes and some of Whistler's finest portraits – for example, *The Little White Girl* (p.24) – although the most celebrated of these is undoubtedly the portrayal of his mother (pp.26-7), which can be found in the Musée d'Orsay, Paris.

Sargent

The most notorious of Sargent's portraits was of Madame Pierre Gautreau (p.92, *Mme X*, Metropolitan Museum, New York), but other prime examples are *Lady Agnew* (p.94, National Gallery of Scotland, Edinburgh), *Miss Palmer* (Colorado Springs Fine Art Centre), and his raffish portrayal of Robert Louis Stevenson (the Taft Museum, Cincinnati, Ohio), which proves that male portraits also came easily to him. Outside portraiture, Sargent is particularly well-represented in Boston – which contains his mural decorations at the Public Library and the finest of his early works, *El Jaleo* (pp.88-9) – and in London. Among the examples to be found there are the best of his plein-air paintings, *Carnation, Lily, Lily, Rose* (p.91, Tate Gallery), and an important collection in oil and watercolour at the Imperial War Museum.

Cassatt

Mary Cassatt's major works are situated, almost exclusively, in American collections, the most impressive selection being in Washington. They include the remarkable *Little Girl in a Blue Armchair* (1878, Mellon Collection, National Gallery of Art), and two fine examples in the Chester Dale Collection, *Girl Arranging her Hair* (1886) and *The Boating Party* (1893-4). Cassatt's earlier paintings reflected the vogue for the Spanish art, and her *Torero and Young Girl* (Sterling and Francine Clark Institute, Williamstown, Massachusetts) is a typical specimen of this.

Hopper

Hopper's most important patron was Gertrude Vanderbilt Whitney. His first one-man exhibition was held at her Studio Club and she continued to offer support throughout his career. As a result, the Whitney Museum of American Art, New York, came to inherit his huge artistic estate of some 2,000 oils, watercolours and prints. In addition, the Museum of Modern Art, in the same city, houses many of his most famous works, among them *Gas* (pp.124-5), *Night Windows* and the best of his theatre paintings, *New York Movie*. Other celebrated pictures include *Nighthawks* (pp.126-7), at the Art Institute of Chicago, and *Sunday*, at the Phillips Collection in Washington. Examples of Hopper's work can be found in many other American museums, but only rarely in Europe. The Thyssen-Bornemisza Collection, Luxembourg is the most notable exception.

BIBLIOGRAPHY

M. Baigell, *A Concise History of American Painting and Sculpture*, Harper & Row, New York, 1984
M. W. Brown, *American Painting from the Armory Show to the Depression*, Princeton University Press, Princeton, 1955
J. M. Carson, *Mary Cassatt*, McKay, New York, 1966
L. Goodrich, *Edward Hopper*, Abradale Press/Harry N. Abrams, New York, 1983
D. Holden, *Whistler Landscapes and Seascapes*, Watson Guptill, New York, 1984
D. F. Hoopes, *The American Impressionists*, Watson Guptill Publications, New York, 1972
H. W. Janson (ed), *American Painting 1900-1970*, Time-Life Library of Art, 1973

G. Levin, *Edward Hopper: The Art and the Artist*, Norton, New York, 1981
K. Lochnan, *The Etchings of James McNeill Whistler*, Yale University Press, New Haven, 1984
D. M. Mendelowitz, *A History of American Art*, Holt, Rinehart & Winston, New York, 1970
S. Olson, *John Singer Sargent*, Macmillan, London, 1986
G. Pollock, *Mary Cassatt*, Park South Books, New York, 1980
C. Ratcliff, *John S. Sargent*, Phaidon, Oxford, 1983
B. Rose, *American Art since 1900*, Thames & Hudson, London, 1975
F. A. Sweet, *Miss Mary Cassatt, Impressionist from Pennsylvania*, University of Oklahoma Press, 1966

OTHER AMERICAN ARTISTS

John James Audubon (1785-1851)
American naturalist, traveller and artist. He studied briefly under David in Paris before going to America in 1803. By 1820 he had turned to making a survey of all the bird species of North America. Finding no publisher for his works there, he came to London to have his famous Birds of America *published from 1827 to 1838 in large folio volumes of hand-coloured aquatints. Many of Audubon's drawings, combining superb draughtsmanship, pure colour and acute observation, are in the New York Historical Society.*

Thomas Hart Benton (1889-1975)
Born in Missouri, Benton trained in Washington and Chicago and at the Académie Julien in Paris. He experimented with Synchromism, but soon abandoned these abstract tendencies to become the spokesman of the Regionalist movement and his best work consisted of important mural commissions in New York, Indiana and Missouri. Something of Benton's dynamism was passed on to his famous pupil, Jackson Pollock.

George Caleb Bingham (1811-79)
American Romantic painter, specializing in frontier scenes. He studied for a time in Philadelphia, but his best pictures were produced after his return to the West in 1844. These include his masterpiece, the stunning Fur Traders Descending the Missouri *(1844, Metropolitan Museum of Art, New York), one of a series of atmospheric paintings depicting life along the river.*

Alexander Calder (1898-1976)
American abstract painter and sculptor. Influenced by Miro in his painting, Calder's ambition was to make 'moving Mondrians' – a form of sculpture called 'mobiles' by Duchamp. His sculptures grew ever larger, reaching 95 feet in his stainless steel Man *for the Montreal Expo '67. There are works by him at Kennedy Airport and in the National Gallery, New York.*

John Singleton Copley (1738-1815)
Although largely self-taught, Copley rapidly established himself as a portraitist in his native Boston, achieving a warm naturalism in works such as The Boy with a Squirrel *(c.1765, Museum of Fine Arts, Boston). In 1774 he settled in London, where his style was influenced by West and Reynolds and, like the former, he specialized in scenes from modern history.*

Charles Demuth (1883-1935)
Demuth was born in Lancaster, Pennsylvania and trained at the Pennsylvania Academy of Fine Arts. He visited Paris where he came to admire the work of Cézanne and Duchamp. From them, he evolved his Precisionist style. Along with the other Precisionists, Demuth celebrated the industrial and agrarian aspects of American life, and his best-known work in this vein is

My Egypt *(1927) which is owned by the Whitney Museum of American Art, New York.*

Thomas Eakins (1844-1916)
Founding father of the American Realist tradition. Eakins was born in Philadelphia but undertook most of his training in Paris. Eakins' interests were not diverted by his European experience and he spent the remainder of his career in Philadelphia, as a lecturer at the Pennsylvania Academy of Fine Arts. There, he introduced the practice of painting from the live model and stressed the importance of anatomical studies. His most famous work, The Gross Clinic *(1875, Jefferson Medical College, Philadelphia) is a compelling reflection of these views, although its gruesome realism shocked his contemporaries. Eakins was also a formative influence on the Ashcan school (see pp.132-5).*

Arshile Gorky (1905-48)
Important transitional figure, linking European Modernist trends with the purely American school of Abstract Expressionism. Born in Turkish Armenia, his parents fled during World War One and the family arrived in the USA in 1920. In the 1940s he evolved a style blending biomorphic, Surrealist forms with the power of Abstract Expressionism. His later life was marred by successive tragedies (including a fire in his studio and a car crash, in which he broke his neck), and he hanged himself in 1948.

Winslow Homer (1836-1910)
Highly versatile painter and illustrator. His early career was spent in New York as an illustrator, producing drawings of the Civil War for Harper's Weekly, and he only devoted himself fully to painting in the 1870s. Homer's broad naturalism developed from the influence of Manet and resulted in such charming pictures as Croquet *(Art Institute, Chicago). His taste for stormy seascapes and rugged depictions of fishermen or hunters competing against the elements led him to settle in lonely, coastal spots – first at Tyneside, in England (1881-2), and later at Prout's Neck, in Maine.*

Roy Lichtenstein (born 1923)
A leading American Pop artist. In his usually large pictures, he parodies commonplace magazine images, often magnifying one or two frames from a cartoon narrative. These he reproduces by hand. Whaam *(1963, Tate Gallery, London) is a typical example. More recently, his focus has shifted to mimicking art – including Picasso and Abstract Expressionism.*

Grandma Moses (Mary Anne Robertson) (1860-1961)
American naive painter. Entirely self-taught, she turned to painting only after the death of her husband when, at the age of 76, arthritis was making it difficult for her to

embroider. The great success of her first one-woman show in New York in 1940 encouraged her to keep painting almost up to her death. Her paintings, marked by their fresh bright colours, are attractive, popular and intimate evocations of country life before 1900.

Georgia O'Keefe (1887-1986)
One of America's major artists and a pioneer of Modernism. Trained in Chicago and New York, she worked at intervals in Texas from 1912 to 1918, where she was much impressed by the landscape. About 1915 she began to make drawings and watercolours that approach abstraction. Her mature abstract style, which emerged by the 1920s, is based on the empty landscapes of the American South-west, its buildings, plant forms and bones, alternating with more representational motifs, such as flowers, as in Black Iris (1926, Metropolitan Museum, New York.)

Jackson Pollock (1912-56)
Leading exponent of the Abstract Expressionist style, Pollock trained under Thomas Hart Benton. His early influences were Surrealism and Indian sand-paintings – both of which can be detected in Guardians of the Secret (1943, San Francisco Museum of Art). Gradually, however, his pictures increased in both size and freedom and, from 1947 to 1953, he produced his famous 'drip' paintings – so-called because the paint was poured rather than brushed onto huge canvases that were pinned to the floor.

Man Ray (1890-1977)
Photographer and painter. Dadaism is evident in paintings such as The rope dancer accompanies herself with her shadows (1916, Museum of Modern Art, New York). Ray was next influenced by Surrealism, exhibiting at the Surrealist Exhibition in Paris in 1925, where he lived from 1920 to 1940. After working in Hollywood as a photographer, he returned to Paris in 1951. His later works are more academic.

Norman Rockwell (1894-1978)
Illustrator and painter. In his paintings of everyday scenes and ordinary people, he normally tells stories, often humorous ones. He won immense popularity as a cover illustrator for The Saturday Evening Post and other magazines. He worked for many advertizers and illustrated the 'Four Freedoms' of the Atlantic Charter in a famous series of paintings.

Mark Rothko (1903-70)
A member of the New York School and one of the creators of Colour Field painting. Largely self-taught, Rothko co-founded 'the Ten', a group of Expressionists, in 1935, although his first important one-man exhibition did not take place until a decade later. His most distinctive style emerged in the 1950s, when he began painting huge canvases with lyrical, floating forms.

Albert Pinkham Ryder (1847-1917)
Uniquely talented American landscape painter. Ryder made several brief excursions to Europe but neither these, nor his surroundings in New York, seem to have made any impact on his art. Instead, his marvellous sea paintings were fired by the memories of his youth in the whaling port of New Bedford, Massachusetts, and by his enthusiasm for Romantic literature. Ryder was largely self-taught and his eccentric technique has unfortunately caused many of his pictures to deteriorate rapidly.

Gilbert Stuart (1755-1828)
With Copley, the most famous American portrait painter of his time. Born in America, he worked abroad until 1792. On his return, he quickly established himself as the leading portraitist of the day, painting leading figures of the new republic. He is most famous for his many portraits of George Washington, and most major American galleries have a Stuart portrait of the President.

Andy Warhol (1928-87)
Painter, film-maker and graphic designer, Warhol was one of the best-known Pop artists. He made his name in 1962 by exhibiting stencilled pictures of Campbell's soup tins, Coca-Cola bottles and Marilyn Monroe, often reproduced by the silk-screen process in multiple images. In the 1960s he produced in his New York studio called The Factory two immensely long and uneventful films, Empire (showing the Empire State Building from one viewpoint for eight hours) and Sleep, six hours of one man asleep. These, with his claim, 'I like boring things', made him the true heir of Dadaism.

Benjamin West (1738-1820)
The first major American painter. West trained briefly in his native Philadelphia, before travelling to Italy in 1760. There he was drawn to the Neo-Classical style, and this formed the basis for his own approach to history painting. In 1763, he visited London – intending it only as a stop-over on his route home – and decided to settle there permanently. His career in England was an unqualified success, as he enjoyed the long-term patronage of George III and eventually, in 1792, succeeded Sir Joshua Reynolds as President of the Royal Academy. Despite his European environment, he also continued to tackle American themes – for example, Penn's Treaty with the Indians (Academy of Fine Arts, Philadelphia).

Grant Wood (1892-1942)
Painter and a leading member of the Regionalist movement. Wood was raised in Cedar City, Iowa, and worked for most of his life in the Mid-West though a trip to Europe, in 1928, fired him with enthusiasm for early Flemish painting and shaped the hard-edged simplicity of his mature style. His best-loved work in this vein is American Gothic (1930, Art Institute, Chicago), which celebrated the homespun virtues of American life. Along with the other Regionalist painters, Wood sought to promote a national school of painting in America.

Andrew Wyeth (born 1917)
One of the most popular contemporary artists, Wyeth has devoted his life to painting the landscape and figures of his Pennsylvanian background and of a small stretch of the Maine coastline. Using watercolour and drybrush, as well as the egg tempera technique he has revived, he employs mainly earth colours with occasional patches of brilliant blue. Christina's World (1948, Museum of Modern Art, New York) is perhaps his best known work.

INDEX

144